JN063424

INTERNATIONAL
SOCIAL WORK
of All People in the Whole World
A NEW CONSTRUCTION

TATSURU AKIMOTO

ARIISW-Shukutoku

Junposha

Published by Junposha
544 Waseda Tsurumakicho, Shinjuku-ku, Tokyo 162-0041, Japan
Copyright ©2024 Tatsuru AKIMOTO,
Asian Research Institute for International Social Work,
Shukutoku University
Printed in Japan

Book design by welle design

ISBN978-4-8451-1870-0

For information, address
Asian Research Institute for International Social Work, Shukutoku University,
200Daiganji-cho, Chuo-ku, Chiba City, Chiba 260-0812, Japan
Tel: +81-(0)43-265-9879
Email: asiainst@soc.shukutoku.ac.jp

Note to readers

This book follows the Hepburn system of romanization.

Long vowels are indicated by macrons (with some exceptions).

Spelling and the use of commas follow the Oxford style, in principle.

On the other hand, the numbering of chapters, sections,

and subsections and the use of double and single quotation marks are

based on the author's own rules.

C o n t e n t s

Chapter One:

Chapter Two:

Dedication

Dedicated to Dr. Maryann Mahaffey, the previous NASW president, and her husband Mr. Hy Dooha, who led me to and in the social work world.

Preface

What is international social work? Is it work that concerns other countries? To do social work in a colony to make it easier to rule, or to be engaged in missionary work or an ODA project as a herald for one's own country's political aggression or economic expansion—is this international social work? Is it international social work to research and introduce to the rest of the world the social welfare situation of any country? Is it to learn from other nations about the solution to problems that immigrants from other countries have, or the improvement of policies and programs of child welfare in one's own country? (Or would this be more national social work?) Is it international social work to be involved with global social issues such as climate change and pandemics, to discuss multiculturalism, or to make international comparisons? Is it international social work to strive for the globalization of Western-rooted social work in the name of a global profession? All of these are not necessarily international social work.

Nearly 100 years have passed since the foundations of international social work were laid. Since then, it has grown into a grand "architecture" due to our predecessors' formidable efforts. These we unconditionally respect and appreciate, and pray that this advancement continues.

These efforts and achievements have been mainly those of the English-medium and/or the Western world. This book is a contribution from the non-English-speaking, non-Western world, which has been neglected. Something new and unique may come out of it.

This book will introduce a new approach to international social work which will be different from prevailing mainstream international social work approaches. This is conceptually to construct a new international social work. It is not to deny, redefine, and reconstruct mainstream international social work.

We think that international social work centres not on certain categories of activities but on a certain "way of viewing matters," which sees things from a perspective outside a nation state (a sovereign nation) including one's own country and/or with "compound eyes" (multiple points of view). The antonym of international social work is national (domestic or local) social work.

The constituency of international social work includes all people(s) of all countries and regions on the Earth. It sees and serves all people equally. To make it a reality, international social work cannot take the equation "Social work = Western-rooted professional social work" for granted. Other types of social work must be also borne in mind if international social work is discussed at all. Western-rooted professional social work has not served, and cannot serve all or the overwhelming majority of the constituency today or in the near future, both in terms of its quantity and quality. International social work must be conformable to all kinds of social work.

International social work does not stop, for example, at the levels of human rights and the United Nations. It further questions their substance. Human rights is not a single-meaning concept. It is also not a peculiar value of international social work but of social work as a whole. The United Nations' organizations, activities, and products are the outcomes of strife among sovereign countries.

The new international social work shows other features. For example:
1. International social work is born twice. Firstly when national borders are drawn up, and secondly, when nation states mature.
2. When nation states mature, there are two ways to overcome their limits or their national borders. One is to have international-related activities of

national social work in a sovereign nation, and the other to have activities (including a view) from the outside of a sovereign nation. Only the latter has been adopted as international social work in our new definition.

3. International social work, which has spun off from (national) social work to be an independent entity out of the sovereignty of nation states and remaining within the framework of social work, reminds us that the element of "being out of the sovereignty of nation states" is inevitable in social work from its birth—as if it were in its genes.

4. International social work is defined not from the "professional (or occupational) social worker" side but from the "social work" side, that is, not from the people who do the social work, but from the beneficiaries of this work.

5. International social work does not simply aim for the globalization of Western-rooted (professional) social work.

(Readers who wish to jump straight to the final definition of the new international social work may refer to Chapter 3.3 from p. 133)

Chapter 1 reviews the achievements of international social work as part of Western-rooted professional social work. Chapter 2 concerns the findings from a study made in a non-English-medium country in the Far East. And based on both chapters, Chapter 3 constructs a new international social work. Chapter 4 gives an example of how the essence of international social work could be conveyed to incoming participants in this field.

This book is composed of four rather independent chapters whose original manuscripts were written in different years over three decades. Chapter 1 mainly in 2021; Chapter 2 in the early 1990s (published in 1995 and 1997); Chapter 3 in 2021-22; and Chapter 4 in the early 2000s (published in 2005). Some out-of-date and inconsistent descriptions among the chapters may be found, but we have kept them to respect and record the original achievements in each year.

The reader may start at any chapter. The repetitive descriptions that occur throughout this book have been retained intentionally for this reason.

Should this book be classified as a textbook, an architectural design, an investigative report, a scholastic academic book, or an essay telling of one man's dream? It does not matter. The author hopes that veteran international social work professors and practitioners enjoy this book with critical sentiment, and anyone who may be interested in international social work will find this book to be the first one their hands alight upon.

Acknowledgements

I am indebted to all my predecessors who dedicated themselves to the development of international social work, particularly, the authors of two specific subsections of the two *Handbooks of International Social Work*, which were published in 2012, Lynne Healy and Nathalie Huegler, Karen Lyons, and Mahohar Pawar. Without their work, this book, particularly its Chapter 1, could never have been realized.

I am also indebted to all the students who attended my international social work classes at various universities in Japan and responded to my assignment in classrooms. Without their contributions, this book, particularly Chapter 4, could not have been possible.

I wish to express my sincere appreciation to my colleagues at the Asian Research Institute for International Social Work (ARIISW), Shukutoku University. Namely, Dr Josef Gohori, Chief Researcher; Ms. Kana Matsuo, Senior Researcher; Dr Masateru Higashida, Head Researcher; and Prof. Yusuke Fujimori, Director of the Asian Buddhist Social Work Center. Discussion with them over a few years was insightful. Particularly, Ms. Matsuo and Dr Higashida kindly read through the whole manuscript at the final stage for the publication and gave valuable comments and suggestions.

The author's special thanks go to Mr. Hiroyasu Kiuchi, President of Junposha, who recognized the meaning and importance of this publication and supported the entire process.

I thank Emily Shibata-Sato and John Burton for their editorial help and support. Finally, I'd like to give special thanks to Mr. Hiroyasu Kiuchi, President of Junposha, who recognized the meaning and importance of this publication and supported the entire process.

Glossary

1 **Activities** (of social workers or those who are engaged in social work): Mainly in Chapter 1, functions, practices, actions, and acts have been interchangeably used in replacement of activities, without strict definitions and discussion on difference and commonality and the relation among them. To excuse the fluidity in the use of terms, the word is enclosed in single quotation marks, as in 'activities.'

2 **Final products**: Definitions. Regarding the use of single quotation marks as in 'a/the final products,' see 1 (**Activities**) above.

3 **Functions** (of social workers; mainly in Chapter 1): See 1.

4 **Idea** (*idee*) (Chapter 3): The meaning here is close to one in philosophy rather than one in daily life—a "thought or suggestion as to a possible course of action." (*Oxford* Dictionary of English, 2nd Ed. Revised, Oxford University Press, 2005)] "The idea (*rinen*) which transcends experiences. The fundamental thought of how the matter is to be." (*Japanese Language Dictionary*, Shōgakukan, 2006) "It is used as the purpose for decision and interpretation without the ontological implication." (*Kōjien*, ver.6, Iwanami Shoten, 2008, 2014). The idea (*idee*) is used in the chapter as a rounding-up concept including a certain way of viewing matters, historical perspective for the future, and dreams (See (a) to (d) on pp.112-114). When used in this meaning, the word is enclosed in single quotation marks as '**Idea** (*idee*).'

5 **International social work**: A general term for social work related to other countries. It can include both international social work (A) (See 6) and international social work (B) (See 7).

6 **International social work (A)** (mainly Chapter 3): International social work as part of national social work. Social work related to other countries

or beyond national borders for one's own country. See 7. Cf. Chapter 3 pp.110.

7 **International social work (B)** (mainly Chapter 3): International social work positioned outside national social work or nation states. Social work that works equally for all people in all countries and regions in the world. See 6. Cf. Chapter 3 pp.110.

8 **International Social Work** (mainly Chapter 3): International social work (B) in the above 7 is replaced with International Social Work (capitalized) to show its authenticity as the international social work we name as such in this book.

9 **International Social Work'** (dash) (Chapter 3, p.119): It is International Social Work in real in an actual society, which is the actual being. A (dash) has been attached to avoid readers' oversight of " ' " a dash.

10 **Local** (mainly Chapter 1): In most cases in this book, it could be replaced with national, domestic, state, or country by country. In some cases, it of course means a particular area within a nation or a country.

11 **Local social work** (mainly Chapter 1): In most cases in this book, it could be replaced with **'national'** social work (mainly Chapter 3); domestic social work; state social work; or social work country by country (See 10 and 15). Regarding the use of single quotation marks as in **'local'** social work or **'state'** social work, see 1 (**Activities**).

12 **Nation** (mainly Chapter 3): It is used as the synonym with state, country, nation state, or sometimes government mostly without strict definition and the discussion on difference and commonality and the relation among them in this book.

13 **National borders** (mainly Chapter 3): It replaces **national boundaries** in Chapter 2 without difference in meaning.

14 **National boundaries** (mainly Chapter 2): See 13. It has been kept respecting the usage in the original article reprinted as a chapter of this book.

15 **National social work** (mainly Chapter 3): Local social work in Chapter 1 is replaced with national social work in Chapter 3 to avoid confusion with the local within a country (See 10) and to clarify the contrast with the international social work outside a country. National social work is also replaceable with domestic social work, state social work, or country-by-country social work. Regarding the use of single quotation marks as in **'national social work,' 'national'** social work, or national **'social work,'** see 1 (**Activities**).

16 **Norm:** See 22. Regarding the use of single quotation marks as in **'norm/s,'** see 1 (**Activities**).

17 **Period** (mainly Chapter 1): The word period is used as a division of historical time sequence (cf. See 18).

18 **Phase** (mainly Chapter 3): The word phase is used as a division of developmental stage in a model (cf. See 17).

19 **Theory of the State** (Chapter 3): It is a nickname given to a model which has a focus on a nation, the birth and development of a nation state, the orientation from welfare state to the welfare world, and does not mean the reference to such grand theories as those of Platōn, Bodin, Spinoza, Rousseau, and Marx. Regarding the use of single quotation marks as in **'a/ the theory of the state,'** see 1 (**Activities**).

20 **TA**: The initial of Tatsuru Akimoto (the current author). It is inserted to indicate his original idea or interpretation input by him (mainly Chapter 1).

21 **Value** (mainly Chapter 1): It could be replaceable for purpose; aim; standard; or ethics in the chapter. Regarding the use of single quotation marks as in **'value,'** see 1 (**Activities**). The content of the value in mainstream social work is defined as e.g., human rights, social justice, democracy, or the promotion of the profession mainly in Chapter 1.

22 **The way of viewing matters**: In Chapters 2 and 3, the value (see 21) in Chapter 1 is replaced by the way of viewing matters, which may be

interchangeably replaced for the way of looking at things; perception; perspective; yardstick; standard; and norm. Regarding the use of single quotation marks as in **'the way of viewing matters,'** see 1 (**Activities**). The content of 'the way of viewing matters' in International Social Work in this book is the view from the outside, not from one's own country, or with multiple views ("compound eyes").

23   **Yardstick**: See 22. Regarding the use of single quotation marks as in **'yardstick,'** see 1 (**Activities**).

Chapter One

A Review of the Conceptual Development of International Social Work in Western-Rooted Social Work
—Understandings of the Term, Concept, and Definition—

This chapter is devoted to the review and interpretation of the conceptual development of understanding of the term, the concept, and definitions of international social work in Western-rooted social work, from its birth to the present day. The purpose of this chapter is to share with readers the common basic knowledge and understanding of the foundation for the discussion on a new construction of international social work in the following chapters. How has the authentic mainstream of international social work been understood throughout its own history? Without this knowledge, no one who would study and/or discuss international social work could move forward.

International social work research seems to have reached a high degree of perfection. Many great works have been amassed. In the last few decades in particular, several extensive volumes have been published, including two books with the same title of *Handbook of International Social Work*, edited by Lyons, K., et al. (Sage Publications, 2012)[1] and by Healy, L. and Link, R. (Oxford University Press, 2012)[2]. Other books in English with the title of *International Social Work* (or with the title including the same words) were written or edited by Hokenstad, M. C. et al. (1992) (1997), Lyons, K. (1999), Healy, L. (2001; 2008; 2021 coauthored by Thomas, R.), Cox, D. and Pawar, M. (2006; 2013), Xu, Q. (2006), Payne, M. and Askeland, G.A. (2008), Hugman, R. (2010) and other authors. Many outstanding journal articles have also been published.

---

1   Particularly, the section "1 Setting the Scene" by Huegler, N., Lyons, K. & Pawar, M., pp.5-13.

2   Particularly, the section "2 Defining International Social Work" by Healy, L. pp.9-15.

The literature review of this chapter is thanks mainly to the above two *Handbooks* and also Lynne M. Healy's *International Social Work: Professional Action in an Interdependent World* (2001; 2020 coauthored by Rebecca L. Thomas, Oxford University Press)[3] listed in the same above paragraph. These works have thoroughly reviewed the earlier literature and succinctly introduced how the term has been used, the concepts, and the representative definitions of international social work. The description of the following sections in this chapter is mostly composed of cited sentences and paragraphs from those books and literature by which they were guided. In that sense, the credit of the literature review in this chapter goes to the original authors of those *Handbooks*, not to the current author.

Cited sentences and paragraphs are dealt with as if they were raw data in field research, and have been edited and interpreted. The editing and interpretation are the current author's. The original data have been assumed to be accurate, appropriate, and sufficient with respect and such a way of treatment would be sufficient and justifiable[4] to achieve the aim of this book which is a new construction of international social work. Carrying out an extensive, complete bibliographical review in itself is not the aim.

Input by the current author (Tatsuru Akimoto) has been intentionally minimized in this chapter to record the authentic history as it is. Exceptions to this have been indicated by the initials, (TA). Examples are the division of periods, the leap from "international" social work to "international social work," the attention to social work at the regional level, the three steps of internationalization/globalization (problems, standards, and practices), and the reference to social background and context.

---

3   Particularly, the section "What Is International Social Work?" pp.5-13 (2001); pp.5-15 2020).
4   A few citations may even be open to the charge of being requotations. The excuse is the accessibility to resources and the lack of availability of time and capacity of the current author, in a non-English medium.

The development will be basically described along a chronological sequence divided into three periods. The main indices for the divisions are the North-South relationship, the incorporation of a value factor, and globalization. The divisions are "1. Up to the 1920s to the Early 40s: Birth and Beginning," "2. The Late 40s to the 80s: Transfer and Assistance from the North to the South," and "3. The 90s to the Early 21st century: Maturity of Definition and International Social Work in Globalization."

1. The Conceptual Development of International Social Work by Period

1.1 Up to the 1920s to the Early 40s: Birth and Beginning

(1) The first usage of the term—the 1928 conference

As far as the current author knows, the first occasion for the term 'international social work' to be used[5] was in 1928 in a presentation by Eglantyne Jebb[6] in the first international social work conference in Paris (Jebb, 1929: 637-657).

Jebb used the term 'international social work' several times in the presentation. The meaning of her international social work was basically international cooperation, particularly through international social institutions such as The Save the Children, The Red Cross, and The International Migration Service. She also emphasized the importance of the[7]

---

5   Huegler, Lyons and Pawar write, "the term 'international social work' was first used in 1943 by Georg Warren" citing (Xu, 2006) (p.10). However, the first use of the term was by Jebb in the 1928 conference and Warren's first use in writing was in 1937 (See 1.1 (3) p.4).

6   "[S]he was unable personally to present her report" due to her illness. "[H]er death occurred soon after the Conference was over." (A footnote of Jebb, 1929: 637; cf. 655-657).

7   She also emphasized their organization and management including the financial aspect (pp. 647-8), and its relationship with national agencies (Jebb, 1929: e.g. 652).

exchange of intellectual research for efficiency, experience, ideas, and suggestions, as well as "special education [for international social work] and constant contact between the international workers" (pp. 651-2, 657). She recognized that the conference itself was one form of such exchanges. (p.652)[8] At the conference, there were "approximately 2,500 [participants] from 42 countries of six continents," including those from the South such as Latin America and Asia. (Healy, 2012: 9) Huegler, Lyon, and Pawar (2012) recognize the conference as adding momentum to the strengthening of the internationalization of social work by these representatives. The present three major international professional organizations, that is, IASSW (International Association of Schools of Social Work), ICSW (International Council on Social Welfare), and IFSW (International Federation of Social Workers) have their roots in this conference. "Subsequently (from the 1920s to the 1940s), social work knowledge and models were also transferred from the North to the South" (Huegler, Lyon and Pawar, 2012: 10).

(2) Before the 1920s

Even before this period, the exchange of information, ideas, and physical visits had been made although the term 'international social work' was not used. International activities "in the form of exchange or transfer of knowledge and practices [were] present in social work from its earliest days. Until the 1920s or so, emerging social work knowledge was mainly shared within the North" (Huegler, Lyon and Pawar, 2012:10).

Not only 'exchange' within the North but also 'transfer of knowledge and models' and 'support and assistance' from the North to the South, which would be largely seen in the following years (see the next subsection (3) below), had been already seen much earlier. Although sections of the books on which we are relying in this chapter have not referred much to the

---

8 She also discussed nationalism, internationalism, and cosmopolitanism as background ideas (pp.637-640, 656).

activities at the regional level, there was much individual and organizational involvement from the North in the South. The expression 'missionary work'—not necessarily being in the religious sense—might often better fit. For example, "Social work was first introduced to Asia before the turn of the 20th century, and some social work programs/schools were established in the second and third decades of the new century" (APASWE, 2013: 1) (TA).

Jebbs also attested to "a rapid and surprising increase in actual international social work," which meant international cooperation through international social organizations, as described in the previous subsection (1), "since the Great War[9]...organization after organization has sprung into being under the pressure of hard necessity" (Jebb, 1929: 650).

(3) The first article—*Social Work Yearbook*, 1937

Russell Sage Foundation's *Social Work Yearbook*, the forerunner of the current NASW *Encyclopedia of Social Work*, had the entry words "International Social Work" for the first time in its Vol.4 in 1937. In previous volumes of the series, there were entries carrying the word "international," namely "International Conferences of Social Work" (Vol. 1, 1929: 229), "International Institutes" (Vol. 2, 1933: 253), and "International Social Case Work" (Vol. 3, 1935: 214), but no entry word "International social work." The content of the latter two (Vols. 2 and 3) pertained to immigrants. The entry word "International Institutes" directed readers to "See Immigrants and Foreign Communities," without any text. "International Social Case Work" (Vol. 3) stated "problems arise in public and private welfare agencies because of the migration of individuals and families to and from the United States" with three subsections: "Nature of problems," "Cooperating agencies," and "The International Migration Services," which had nine offices in European cities

---

9   WWI

and New York (Vol. 3, 1935: 214).[10] In Vol. 4 (1937), under the first entry word of "International Social Work", George Warren wrote that "International social work is composed of the following three activities. (p.224)" (Akimoto, 1995: 98; 1997: 26):

(a) international social case work; (b) international conferences on social work subjects; (c) international cooperation by governments and private bodies under the auspices of the League of Nations, the International Labour Organization and the League's Health Organization in the world-wide efforts to combat disease, improve conditions of labor, and to protect women and children (Warren, 1937).

The next Vol. 5 (1939: 192) had four activities instead of the previous three, adding, between (a) and (b) above, "(b) International assistance, public and private, to disaster or war sufferers and distressed minority groups." The earlier (c) above was rewritten as "(d) the international cooperation by governments and private bodies through the medium of the League of Nations. The International Labour Organization and the Health Organization of the League, in combatting disease and securing social and political peace and harmony throughout the world."

In this period or even in the earlier years, most kinds of international social work activities which would be seen in later periods were already presented: exchange and transfer; service and assistance to migration, war, and disaster suffers and distressed minority groups; international cooperation through intergovernmental organizations such as the League of Nations and the ILO (International Labour Organization), and INGOs

---

10   It is composed of three subsections, "Nature of problems," "Cooperating agencies," and "The International Migration Services" which had nine offices in European cities and New York (Vol. 3, 1935: 214-216).

(international nongovernmental organizations) work, including professional social work organizations. Their main activities seemed to focus on activities within the North (and cases, incidents, and challenges related to their own countries), but some involvement in and of the South was already observable.

1.2 The Late 40s to the 80s: The Transfer and the Assistance from the North to the South, and the Leap from "International" Social Work to "International Social Work" (TA)

(1) The immediate postwar period and following decades, and the North-South problem with the East-West relationship behind (TA)

"During the 1940s and 1960s, and particularly following the Second World War, a particular kind of international social work peaked, in terms of transfer of education, practice and welfare models and skills…" It was "mostly from the North to the South," the "linear flow," "with support from UN organizations and INGOs, and respective governments of new nation states" (Huegler, Lyons and Pawar, 2012: 11). The Asian and Pacific Association for Social Work Education (APASWE)'s history publication begins with the following sentences (TA):

> [V]arious social work-related activities were carried out and workshops, training seminars, and conferences were organized in the Region by non-Asian agencies, most typically from the United Nations and United States. Some other international organizations along with the United Kingdom, a previous colonial power, were involved as well as people from other Western countries. These same entities and individuals initiated new schools and supported them in many countries (APASWE, 2013: 1).

In the Asian region, the first schools of social work were established in 1944 in Thailand, in 1946 in Indonesia, in 1950 in The Philippines, in 1952 in Malaysia and Sri Lanka, although in India its first school had been established in 1936 (Matsuo, 2015: 74).

As far as this particular period and the following few decades are concerned, it is worth looking at the social situation of those years to understand international social work at that time. Just after World War II, the United States was active (directly and through the United Nations and NGOs), in aid in political, economic, and social arenas for postwar rehabilitation in the broad region, first including Europe.

By the 1970s, more than 80 new countries had gained their independence, mainly in Asia and Africa, and some in Latin America. This independence was the denial of the rule of previous colonial suzerain states such as the United Kingdom, France, and some other mainly European countries, and the liberation from the old imperialism. Independence did not eliminate all problems. The mass poverty and other serious political, economic, and social problems continued and sometimes even worsened. The North-South problems co-existed with the East-West or socialism vs. capitalism issue. Competition intensified between the West and the East and among the new Western or Northern powers (new imperialism). ODA (Official Development Assistance) was one of its representative examples. (TA) Under these conditions, on one hand, social work spread all over the world due to the profession's own efforts. Social work regional associations were born from within IASSW, firstly in Latin America in 1967, secondly in Africa in 1971, and thirdly in Asia in 1974 (APASWE, 2013: 1). On the other hand, the dissemination of social work was limited to a certain level, due to the negative reaction against the reformist approach offered by the West or the North. 'Placation measures by American imperialism,' or 'preventive measures against socialist revolution,' were words sometimes hurled against social work among "undeveloped" countries as well as within some "developed" countries (TA).

This period stands out as the time of transfer and assistance from the

North to the South, not only knowledge and skills but also models of social work itself. The North's social work was involved in various direct practices, consultative and advocacy roles in policy and program development, and program and curriculum development in social work education in the South.

(2) Narrow definitions and broad definitions

In the 1950s and later, the territory of international social work, or what international social work was, was more consciously discussed. Some preferred a narrow/specific territory or definition and some others a broad/general territory or definition. The working committee of the Council on Social Work Education (CSWE) of the United States (1956), and Sanders and Pederson (1984) were deemed to be the two poles. The former chose a narrow definition and the latter a broad one. The former confined itself to programs by the United Nations, governmental or non-governmental agencies. The latter opted for "social work activities and concerns that transcend national and cultural boundaries" (Sanders and Pederson, 1984: xiv). Healy introduces citations to support each position as well as those in between.

For the former:

> [CSWE's] working committee members wrestled with the question of narrow versus broad interpretation and examined six different usages of the term..., "ranging from social workers working in other countries to refugee services to common professional concerns with social workers in other parts of the world" (Healy, 1995: 423).

> The committee opted for a narrow definition..."[T]he term 'international social work' should properly be confined to programs of social work of international scope, such as those carried on by intergovernmental

agencies, chiefly those of the U.N.; governmental; or non-governmental agencies with international programs (Stein, 1957: 3)" (Healy, 2001: 5-6).

For the latter:

At the most general level, international social work can be defined as any aspect of the profession that involves more than one country. This draws on the dictionary definition of *international* as meaning 'of, relating to or affecting two or more nations' and 'active, known or reaching beyond national boundaries' (Marriam-Webster, 2011) (Healy, 2012: 10).

Kimberly (1984) argued that international social work, as a relatively new field, should be left open for broad interpretation rather than prematurely limiting its scope (Healy, 2001: 6).

There could be various definitions with different widths between these two. At the very end of the 1980s, Healy conducted a study of 11 Social Work (IASSW) member schools, yielding 200 responses from all 5 regions (1989/90) to "identify the component concepts…essential to the definition of international social work." (Healy, 2001: 6) It listed various presumable international social work activities for schools' selection:

Respondents…selected the following concepts as essential, in descending order: cross-cultural understanding, comparative social policy, concerns with global issues, a general worldwide view, knowledge of a common profession worldwide, international practice, intergovernmental social welfare, and a sense of collegiality with social workers in other countries (Healy, 1990)…[C]ross-cultural understanding [collected the biggest votes] (Healy, 2001: 6-7).

(3) Four points to keep in mind for further discussion

While "[l]ittle was written about practice roles during this period [the 1970s and 1980s]" (Healy, 2012: 10), there are four points to be kept in mind in this period for future discussion. (TA)

The first one is Goldman's idea in the early 1960s and unique "to define international social work as the fourth major practice method to complement casework, group work, and community organization." Goldman (1962) proposed as a logical step in expanding social work attention beyond the community level to seek 'international solutions to international problems' (pp.1-2), much as a caseworker seeks individual solutions to problems of individuals" (Healy, 2012:11). There was no progress on this idea in later periods.

The second and the third points are the attention paid to the general ideas of the importance of an international perspective, and partly related to this, the importance of comparative study. Both will be the focus of the interest of more disputants (e.g. Lyons, 1999: 12). In this period, "Boehm (1976) loosely defined international social work as including the obvious work of international agencies but also comparative analysis and its contribution to the transnational exchange of ideas and innovations" (Healy, 2012: 10).

The fourth is criticism of the "unidirectional," "linear flow," transfer and support (aid and assistance) from the North to the South: "professional imperialism"[11] (Midgley, 1981). To some social workers, the word "imperialism" might sound abrupt, but was nothing peculiar outside of the social work field in the social context of that time, as seen in the above subsection (1.2 (1) p.22). We, however, read this criticism as an impetus having an important

---

11 Cf. "cultural imperialism" (Midgley, 1983) (Lyons, 1999: 17) The warning of social work colonialism was also repeatedly sent to the chorus of professionalization, internationalization, and globalization in "developing countries" in these few decades on various occasions including international conferences and workshops (e.g., Akimoto, in Indonesia (2013), Vietnam (2014), and Thailand (2015)).

effect on international social work. (See the next section 1.3 (2) p. 31, 2 (1) (ii) pp.44-47) (TA).

1.3 The 1990s to the Early 21st Century: Maturity of Definition and International Social Work in Globalization

Two points feature in this period. On one hand, the reference and discussion on 'what international social work is' became active in the form of a definition. While definitions based on activities, acts, practices, or functions (hereinafter to be referred to as either 'activities' or 'functions' in this section) had come close to maturity, definitions based on values, purposes, aims, goals, standards, or ethics (hereinafter to be referred as mainly 'value' in this section) emerged and became popular.

On the other hand, in the 1990s, the term 'globalization' emerged and gradually replaced 'internationalization' although the two terms significantly differ in meaning.

The reference and discussion on international social work's relation to 'local' (or domestic, national, state; hereinafter to be referred to as 'local' in this section) social work became unavoidable.

(1) Towards the maturity of functional definitions

(1-1) Falk and Nagy's survey: 12 classifications of international social work knowledge and activities

Falk and Nagy conducted a survey in 1995/96 to give "rise to a wide range of ideas about the 'meaning' of international social work" (Huegler, Lyons, and Pawar, 2012: 11). The subjects were 800 schools of social work in 20 countries in Europe, North America, and Australia. The response rate was 50 percent. "The following is a summary of their classification of international social work knowledge and activities (derived from respondents' views)" (Lyons,

1999: 26) (cf. Falk and Nagy, 1997):

1. International events and social forces that generate the problems faced by the world's peoples
2. The implications of the increasing interdependence of nations
3. The role of international governments and NGOs
4. The increasing influence of multinationals and global financial organizations
5. Comparative social policies, structures, values, and cultural assumptions
6. Practice approaches, programmes, and methods used in other cultures
7. The range of international practice opportunities
8. Struggles for a more just world and support for human rights
9. Working with immigrants and refugees in one's own country
10. Educational exchanges for educators, students, and practitioners
11. International consultation projects
12. International seminars and conferences.

Items 1 to 6 pertain to "knowledge" which international social work should be equipped with while items 7 to 12 to "activities" which international social work would be engaged in.

(1-2) Healy's definition: A representative functional definition

In 2001, Healy gave a representative definition of international social work which was based on the review of the various works including ones cited above, particularly ones providing categories of practice activities. She named it the functional or practice-based definition. This was consistent with the trend since 1937 Warren's Year Book article (1(3) p.4), which continued in the early decades of the twenty-first century. A feature of Healy's definition here was the reference to "international policy development and advocacy," and not only direct practice.

International professional action and the capacity for international action by social work profession and its members.[12] International action has four dimensions: (a) internationally related domestic practice and advocacy, (b) professional exchange, (c) international practice, and (d) international policy development and advocacy (Healy 2001: 7). (The letters (a) to (d) are the insertion by the current author.)

The definition comprises "four dimensions of action" ((a) to (d)) by the profession and professional social workers (Healy, 2012: 10). She gives these with the following examples for each dimension (Healy 2001: 7-13):

(a) Internationally related domestic practice and advocacy: "Refugee settlement, work with other international populations, international adoption work, and social work in border areas." (p.7)

(b) Professional exchange: "To exchange social work information and experiences internationally, and to use the knowledge and experience to improve social work practice and social welfare policy at home." "Reading foreign periodicals and books in one's field, corresponding with professionals in other countries or hosting visitors, participating in professional interchange at international meetings, and identifying and adapting social welfare innovations in other countries to one's own settings." (p.9)

(c) International practice: "To contribute directly to international development work through employment and volunteer work in international development agencies." (p.10)

(d) International policy development and advocacy: "A worldwide

---

12   The phrase "to promote human dignity and human rights and enhance human well-being" was inserted later in the third version of her same book. (Healy, 2020: 8) See (2-2) p.33-34.

movement to formulate and promulgate positions on important social issues and make a contribution to resolution of important global problems related to its sphere of experience." (p.12) (e.g. domestic violence, women's status; "The goal of the educational effort was to influence UN policy deliberations.") (p.13)

(1-3) Hugman's classification of practices of international social work

Reviewing definitions that had been proposed, Hugman neatly presented international social work practice and work in the form of five categories made from the combination of the locations of social workers and clients and the problems they are engaged in (Hugman, 2010: 18-20):

(1) The practice of social work in a country other than the home country of the social work;

(2) Working with individuals, families and communities whose origins are in a country other than that where the social worker is practicing;

(3) Working in international organizations;

(4) Collaborations between countries in which social workers exchange ideas or work together on projects that cross national borders; and

(5) Practices that address locally issues that originate in a globalized social system.

Items (1) to (4) are often commonly found in definitions we cited in previous sections, but item (5) is not. Noting the globalization of social issues and problems as a connecting factor between social work providers and beneficiaries, Hugman gives the following definition:

'International social work' refers to practice and policy concerning[13] situations in which professionals, those who benefit from their services or

---

13   "and"?

[sic] the causes of the problems that bring these two actors together, have travelled in some way across the borders between nations (Hugman, 2010: 20).

(2) Incorporation of the value factor

Up until this period, international social work was mainly defined around the kinds or the categories of activities or functions by social workers, broadly or narrowly, but some authors focused on 'value' in their definitions.

(2-1) Haug's definition: A value-focused definition

Item 5 of Falk and Nagy (1997)'s 12 classifications above ((1-1) p. 28) had the word 'value' in it. "Ahmadi (2003) called for focusing or refocusing international social work on promotion of human rights, democracy, social justice, conflict prevention, and peace" (Healy, 2012: 11). Haug (2005) also "focus[ed] on common goals and values such as a clear commitment to human rights and social justice" (p.132) in her definition:

> International social work includes any social work activity anywhere in the world, directed toward global social justice and human rights, in which local practice is dialectically linked to the global context (Haug, 2005: 133).

Instead of 'value,' each writer does and could use a different term—aim, purpose, goal, standard, perspective, or ethics. The content of 'value' could be also of a verity. The 'value' in Haug's definition is social justice and human rights, but Ahmadi above, for example, adds democracy, conflict prevention, and peace, while Cox and Pawar added ecology and social development under the name of perspective (Cox and Pawar, 2013: 29-30; (2-2) p.33-34).

Haug's short definition implies a few important points. First, it begins with the clause "International social work includes any social work activity anywhere in the world." This statement seems not to limit the subject, or the player, of international social work merely to professional social workers as far as we can see in these three lines above, although it is not clear if it limits the work to social workers. Most of the definitions cited in this chapter define international social work as some categories of activities by professional social workers and/or as those to promote social work profession, including Healy's definition above and Cox and Pawar's definition below.[14] Haug's clause also clarifies the object, or the target population, of international social work, to be all people anywhere in the world. Most other definitions would share the same idea but their expression is less clear and direct. Cox and Pawar's in the next subsection reads "(the wellbeing of) large sections of the world's population" and Healy's and Hugman's definitions above partly start with the social worker's own people.

Secondly, Haug's definition ends with the clause "local practice is dialectically linked to the global context." It has shown the interest in the relation of local practice under globalization, which will be discussed in the next subsection (3) below.

Thirdly, are "social justice and human rights" appropriate as the 'value' of international social work even if she inserts "global" in front of them? They are core elements of the typical Western-rooted professional social work,[15] which the author of the same article was critical about. She argued this point extensively in the first half of the same article including her definition above (Haug, 2005). It is difficult to "get out of the hands of Western-rooted professional social work."

---

14   Their inclusion of professional building is in keeping with developments by the international professional associations to promulgate a global definition, ethical guidelines, and an action agenda for social work from local to global levels, the Global agenda for Social Work and Social Development (Healy, 2020:7).

15   cf. IASSW/IFSW Global Definition of Social Work Profession.

These discussions, however, mostly pertain to the understanding and definition of social work itself, not those of international social work, strictly speaking.

(2-2) Cox and Pawar's definition and Healy's revised definition: Combined (functional and value-focused) definition

Cox and Pawar give a long definition emphasizing "the promotion of social work education and practice" and aims at "building a truly integrated international profession."

International social work is the promotion of social work education and practice globally and locally, with the purpose of building a truly integrated international profession that reflects social work's capacity to respond appropriately and effectively, in education and practice terms, to the various global challenges that are having a significant impact on the wellbeing of large sections of the world's population. This global and local promotion of social work education and practice is based on an integrated-perspectives approach that synthesizes global, human rights, ecological, and social development perspectives of international situations and responses to them (Cox and Pawar, 2013: 29-30; cf. 2006: 20).

This definition seems to be between Healy's functional definition and Haug's value-focused definition. Healy reads this definition to fit "within the category of a functional definition" "with its action and practice emphasis," "but it also includes…value dimensions," "with the purpose of building a truly integrated international profession" (Healy, 2012: 11). The 'value' has been replaced with perspectives which integrate not only human rights but also ecology and social development.

The discussion on the subject, the object, and the 'value' in subsection (2-1) (pp.31-33) under Haug's definition is also applicable to Pawar. Pawar pointed out the "Northern contexts reflecting Northern concerns" in those definitions discussed above (Pawar, 2010) (cf. Huegler, Lyons and Pawar, 2012: 12).

Functions and value factors are combined in definitions of international social work. Healy, for example, inserted a phrase in her definition, a phrase "to promote human dignity and human rights and enhance human well-being," at the end of the first sentence of her definition above in the third version of her book. (See the above (1-2) p.29). "[I]nternational social work is value-driven action aimed at promoting human rights and human well-being globally" (Healy, 2020: 15).

(3) Globalization and social work: International social work's relation with 'local' social work

The literature review pages of the books which we have been relying on have mostly a focus on the 'globalization.'[16]

(3-1) Social work under globalization

Everything comes under globalization. Social work alone cannot be exempted. "All social work is enmeshed in global processes of change" (Lorenz, 1997:2). The globalization of social work seems to be in three layers: (a) The globalization of the realities; (b) the globalization of standards; and (c) the globalization of practice[17] (TA) (cf. Akimoto, 1992).

(a) Globalization of realities: "Globalization has led to new social problems and increased awareness of others that have long existed; increasingly, these problems are experienced in most or even all countries." Payne

---

16   The conscious discussion on the difference of 'globalization' from 'internationalization' is not cited. Questions and discussions parallel to those raised here in this subsection must be also made on 'internationalization' (TA).

17   "Theory," not "practice," in the original article (Akimoto, 1992: title, etc.).

34

and Askeland (2008) discuss "the growing inequality and injustice [as] the result from globalization" from their postmodern point of view (Healy, 2012: 10, 11).

(b) Globalization of standards: "Standards in human rights are increasingly negotiated at the global level and social provisions and programs are modelled and emulated across borders." (Healy, 2008). Haug (2005) also specified social justice and human rights as standards (1.3 (2-1) p.31). "Human rights" is also found in the above-cited Ahmadi (2003) and Cox and Pawar (2013). (1.3 (2-1) p.31 and (2-2) p.33).

(c) Globalization of practice: "[G]lobal trends in every sphere of life—economy, security, health, environment, and culture—affect social work practice, practitioners, and clients of social work interventions" (Healy, 2012:10).

All social problems or social work needs are in the global context and are affected by the element of 'globalization.' Standards are also the same. Both clients[18] who have faced problems and social workers who work for them must have recognized and understood these facts and also the fact that their cases or practices themselves are under the same globalization.

(3-2) 'Local' social work under globalization

All social work comes under globalization. 'Local' social work cannot be exempted and is in the same three layers immediately above. In other words, the element of 'being in the global context' penetrates all aspects and every corner of 'local' social work. 'Local' practice must be seen through an international lens.

---

18   The term 'client' is not acceptable for many social workers. We will, however, use it for the easier understanding of the line of thought.

[I]ncreasing numbers will find it necessary to develop their comparative knowledge of welfare systems and social work services if they are to engage in transnational activities in specialist areas of work which might previously have been seen as restricted to the national scene, e.g. transnational fostering (Lyons, 2006) (Huegler, Lyons, and Pawar, 2012: 12).

In not only the transnational cases but also 'purer domestic' cases, more generally, "applications of international perspectives to local practice" become requisite (Akimoto, 2020:42).

Lyons et al. (2006) and Lawrence et al. (2009)…suggest that local practices can—and should—be viewed through an international lens or that knowledge about international events and different cultures should inform local practices (Huegler, Lyons, and Pawar, 2012: 12).

"[L]ocal and national borders are no longer sufficient limits for our information sources and ethical practice" (Link and Ramanathan, 2011: 1). "These shared social problems and the movement of people across borders challenges the very notion of a domestic social work practice" (Healy, 2012: 10). "[L]ocal practice is dialectically linked to the global context" (Haug, 2005: 133; (2-1) p.31). The word 'dialectic' would promise the 'local practice' which is rather different from the existing 'local practice'—synthesis on thesis and antithesis (TA).

(3-3) Discussing not '(local) social work under globalization' but 'international social work under globalization' (TA)—Will international social work disappear?

These discussions in this subsection, however, all seem to pertain to ('local') social work, or ('local') social work in the global context, and not to what international social work is ((2-1) p.31), which we have been examining. It is similar to the discussions on professional social work, Western social work bias, and the equation of the 'value' = 'human rights and social justice' in the previous subsection. ((2-1) p.31). We will have to focus on international social work under globalization.

1) Will international social work disappear? If the answer is "no," what, then, will it look like?

On one hand, it could be said that ('local') social work absorbs international social work into it. If the element of 'global' penetrates all aspects and every corner of 'local social work,' and all social workers need to understand and have the view of international social work, how do we distinguish international social work from globalized 'local social work'? According to this logic, will the field of practice/research of international social work become unnecessary and cease to exist? The following citation has supposed that international social work will, in practice, remain.

> [W]hile not all social workers will choose to engage in 'international social work' as a specialist activity...the internationalization of social problems will require increasing numbers of social professionals [sic][19] to have knowledge about international conditions and current affairs in order to understand the concerns of the service users and respond appropriately (Huegler, Lyons, and Pawar, 2012: 12).

At least two out of four areas in Healy's definition ((1-2) p.29), that is, "(c) international practice, and (d) international policy formulation and advocacy" might be kept for international social work.

---

19 "social work professions"?

Not all social workers will become international social workers and be equipped with knowledge about international conditions and current affairs at the same level as international social workers. The lens mentioned above ((3-2) p.36) is one of 'globalization' or 'global context,' and not one of international social workers.

What will the roles and functions of international social work be? What will the meaning, concept, and definition of international social work look like? The discussion has not proceeded beyond these questions yet.

2) What will it be like if the answer is "yes", that is, if international social work disappears?

On the other hand, there are a few ideas questioning the retention of 'international social work' in the future. Lyons wrote that international social work "is a nebulous concept" while mentioning "elements of cross-national comparison and applications of international perspectives to local practice, as well as participation in policy and practice activities which are more overtly cross-national or supra-national in character" (Lyons, 1999:12). Huegler, Lyons, and Pawar, (2012: 12) noted:

> There are also those within the North who question the appropriateness of the term 'international social work' and argue for more work to develop a theory and practice that examine processes and the diverse ways in which the global and the local interact (e.g. Dominelli, 2010)[20] or who advocate the notion of social work internationalism, rather than international social work (Lavalette and Ioakimidis, 2011).

---

20 Being invited to a forum (The Fourth ARIISW-Shukutoku-University International Academic Forum, February, 2021, at Chiba, Japan) to discuss the future of international social work, she focused on the increase and the importance of global social issues such as climate change and COVID 19 pandemics.

It may be worth remembering, lastly, Webb's argument to "reject the validity of an international or global social work."

> "[S]ocial work is inherently local and requires deep understanding of local culture," therefore social work "has no clearly identified or legitimate mandate in relation to globalization" and "'global social work' is a practical impossibility" (p.193) and no more than a vanity for the profession (Webb, 2003: Huegler, Lyons, and Pawar, 2012:11).

We wonder if Webb would keep the same insistence if replacing "globalization" and "global social work" with "internationalization" and "international social work." Unfortunately, he did not distinguish between international social work and global social work as far as his quoted lines above are concerned.

Meanwhile, in this period, various forms of international social work activities—starting with 'exchange'—have continued to increase. Healy comments, "Communication technologies facilitate rapid and frequent exchange of ideas across the globe and access to information about local and global developments." "The profession is continuing to mature and develop in a highly globalized context" (Healy, 2012: 10).

2. Roundup and Limitations

(1) A summary of the conceptual development of international social work by period

We have reviewed the entire development of meanings, concepts, and definitions of international social work from its birth to today, chronologically dividing it into three periods in the previous section. These will be summarized in Table 1-1 below with some current author's analytic interpretation added.

The first column is the division of those periods: Period I (Up to the end of the 20s to the early 40s), Period II (the second half of the 40s to the 80s), and Period III (the 90s to the early 21st century). The second column is the developmental stage of the term/concept/definition of international social work: Birth-Growth-Mutuality (and Re-examination). The third column is 'Events' (publication and social background). The fourth column contains representative activities practiced under the name of international social work and some explanatory remarks. The last column on the right is the North-South relation and the main supposed beneficiaries which characterize each period.

(i) Period I: Birth and infancy

Period I refers to the birth and infancy of the term 'international social work.' This was from the end of the 1920s to the early 1940s, but virtually to the end of the 30s due to the World War.

The term international social work made its appearance in Jebbs' paper for the 1928 Paris international social work conference, and Warren's article in the 1937 *Social Work Year Book* Vol.4. These authors referred to activities in several categories under the name of international social work.

These categories can be summarized as follows: 1. international cooperation among governments, (e.g. the League of Nations and ILO) and non-governmental agencies (e.g. Save the Children and Red Cross); 2. the exchange of information, knowledge, skills, experiences, and ideas including international conferences; and 3. the casework and assistance to migrants, war and disaster victims, and distressed minority groups.

These activities were mostly carried out in and among the Northern, social work-developed countries. The main motivation was in learning and benefiting themselves as individuals or agencies in their own countries, and/

or in providing good services and assistance to people relating mainly to their own countries. Some interest was also shown in helping people and disseminating social work in non-North regions.

In the years (from the 19th century to the 1920s) before Period I, some of these activities were carried out in the North and/or non-North out of "goodwill" and as "missionary work" (not necessarily a religious sense) without being called international social work. It was the period of prehistory.

During this period, the term international social work was mostly used as "international" social work, which meant social work related to or concerning matters "international."

Table 1-1. The historical development of the understanding, concept, and

	Period	The development of term/concept/definition		Events [Publication and social background]
	(Prehistory) 19c-the end of the 1920s	No terms, no concepts		
I	The end of the 1920s- the early 40s	The Birth of the term and Infancy *"International" social work (SW related to "international")*		1928 Paris Conference (Jebbs) 1937 SW Year Book Vol. 4 (Warren)
II	The 2nd half of the 40s-the 80s	Growth *"International" social work* ⇩ *"International social work" (An independent concept)*		[Immediate postwar; Independence of previous colonies] [North-South problems] [East-West relations] [Internationalization]
III	The 90s- the early 21c	III-A	Maturity towards the final product *Incorporation of value factor*	 2001 Healy 2005 Haug 2020 Healy; 2006 Cox & Pawar
		III-B	Reexamination of the concept ISW Prosperity or dissolution	[Globalization]

42

definition of international social work by period

Representative ISW activities/explanatory remarks	North-South relation [For whom]
Virtual international social work activities following the nomenclature in the later periods (from e.g. "Goodwill"; "Missionary obligation"; Intellectual/practical interest)	North→Non-North [others]
Exchange (intellectual ideas; conferences); Organizational cooperation (INGO, UL, ILO, etc.); International research; Case work (immigrants), Assistance to war, disaster victims, and depressed minority people, etc. by social workers	Within the North [Self/own country]

Assistance/Aids (relief and development); Transfer of models
     The criticism of the North-South (unidirectional;
    power differential; unequal) relations; imperialism
 The exploration of the concept/definition
 The extraction and combination of various categorized activities (functions)
 →International perspective; Comparative studies; Cross cultural perspective
	Within the North
	 North→South [others; South]
	
	 (South-South)

Pursuing the final definition—"What is ISW?"
     Correction of unidirectional→Bidirectional; equal→
     Value in general→Filling its content (e.g. human rights,
    social justice, democracy, and the promotion of
    professional social work)
 • Functional definition (Certain categorized functions/ activities by professional social workers)
 • Value-focused definition (purpose; aim; standard)
 • Combined function-and-value-focused definithon
	North=South (Bidirectional; equal) [Both North and South] At least in theory

→Social work is globalized. The whole 'local' social work is put in the global context. →All 'local' social works must be seen through lens of "global". ISW will be more prosperous. Or will disappear?	Centre→Peripheries (North→South) [All or uni-polar]

(ii) Period II: Growth—from "international" social work to "international social work"

Period II runs between the latter half of the 40s and the 1980s, which includes the immediate postwar period (when rehabilitation aid was given to the North as well as the South, by the North); the decades of the independence of former colonies; and the emergence of the Third World and North-South problems. The transfer of knowledge, skills, and models of social work was made from the North to the South, and the financial and technological assistance and support in practice, policy formulation, and education were given in and for the South by the North. These became the major forms of international social work activities in this period. In the background, there were East-West relations.

In the face of this unidirectional move, criticism of imperialism and colonialism was raised. Towards the end of this period, the international social work side made some responses to this criticism.

Period II was also the time when the concept of "what 'international social work' is," or its core elements and definitions began to be explored. "International" social work, which comprised of two terms, 'international' and 'social work', turned into "international social work," which was one independent term or concept, at some point during this Period. The major trend was the extraction of the elements and the combination of various categorized activities (functions, acts, practices; hereinafter to be referred to as activities in this section).

Internationalization, which became a popular word worldwide, brought to social work the international perspective, international comparative perspective, and cultural perspective. International comparative studies and cross-cultural counselling, for example, became popular subjects in international social work research and practice.

However, the conceptual or definitional development of international social work was slow during this period, except for the leap from "international" social work to "international social work," while there was much cross-national activity and growth in terms of social work practice and education.

(iii) Period III: Maturity to the final definition and self reexamination

Period III (The 1990s to the early 21st century) is characterized by two features: firstly, (A) the maturity of the definition of international social work, and (B) the re-examination of the understanding of international social work due to globalization.

(A) Looking at (A), Period III was the succession of Period II in terms of North and South relations, but the unidirectional relationship from North to South in the previous period was gradually corrected into a two-directional or horizontal relationship—the recognition of mutual relation, interdependence, mutual learning and sharing, and the acquisition of the eyes of parity—between the two, in theory. In reality, however, the power difference certainly remained. A historical background event in this period was the mitigation of East-West relations.[21*]

The conceptual pursuit of 'what international social work is' continued towards and approached its final form. There were two trends—one conventional and one new.

The conventional trend was the exploration of the elements and categories of activities/functions of international social work which succeeded from Phase II, even some from Period I. Over them, definitions basically developed—from Warran to Healy ('functional definitions').

The new trend which replaced 'function' with 'value' (purpose aim, standards, and ethics; hereinafter to be referred as 'value'), emerged in the middle of the first decade of the 21st century (e.g. Haug). The 'value' most representatively meant human rights and social justice, sometimes

---

21*   In around the 2020s, a new China and Russian-Western relationship is emerging.

democracy, the promotion of professional social work, development, ecology, and others ('value-focused definitions').

In later years, both the functional definition and the value-focused definition merged, in some definitions. Healy's (revised) (2010) was a representative model. Cox and Powar's (2006) was interpreted as one of these definitions.

The criticism of professional imperialism raised in Phase II to the reality of international social work was from the outside of these definitions. It turned to a necessary definitional component to be international social work. It is not the international social work unless the component is included (cf. Box 1-1).

Period III was a time of the correction of the 'unidirectional' and the incorporation of the 'value' judgement factor, and the finalization of the product (definition).

(B) Looking at (B), Period III was also the time of globalization. The above discussion in (A) and the following discussion in this (B) proceeded at a time, not in sequence, in Period III.

Society was globalized and social work was globalized. All 'local' (national, state, or domestic) social works were put in the global context. The 'global' element penetrated every corner of 'local' social work. As a result, everything in social work had to be seen with "global" eyes or lenses—with the understanding that everything is in such a global world. Problems, standards, and practices are all globalized. International social work will increase its own importance more and more. Or international social work will conceptually disappear, being absorbed and swallowed by 'local' social work. The concept of international social work itself is requestioned.

The features of each Period sometimes overlap. Some characters and elements of a Period may appear in earlier Periods, and characters and elements of earlier Periods continue appearing in later Periods.

Digression for the intellectually curious

Box 1-1. Hypothetical logical progress from a criticism to a value

The criticism of professional imperialism and social work colonialism, which were born in Phase II, is one of the driving forces that led to the incorporation of a value factor into the concept and definition of international social work. It was hypothetically developed as follows:

1. It criticized the unidirectional North-South relationship and power differential.
2. This meant that a value judgemental factor was brought into the international social work discussion.
3. In the later years of Period II, criticism sought a correction to the bidirectional relationship between North and South, and extended the interest to the broader, general issues, e.g., interdependency, mutual benefit, and mutual sharing, that is, to the concept of equality in general.
4. These qualities are common in social work in general, but not particularly so to international social work. Particular to international social work is that the subjects of equality are between and among countries, peoples, and individuals beyond national borders.
5. Once equality becomes a general term, it is easily expanded to become a value, which is a more extensive general concept.
6. In the process from 1. to 3. and from 3. to 5., the original interest and focus of the criticism of power differences and mass poverty (the North-South relationship) becomes diluted in a sense. The coverage becomes broader, and the aim becomes diluted and euphemistic.

There is no factual and historical connection between the criticism of professional imperialism in Period II and the incorporated 'value' factor in Period III. However, it would be possible to trace a logical and hypothetical connection, from the criticism to the 'value.'

(2) The final definitions of international social work

(i) Basic structure: Categorical activities × Professional social workers (a function-focused definition)

Almost all these understandings of the concept including definitions seem to be the aggregation or partial combination of categorized activities, which professional social workers have been engaged in. Those activities range from (a) the exchange and transfer of information, knowledge, ideas, skills, and models, including mutual visits and conferences, (b) practices related to overseas at home countries, (c) practices in other countries, (d) assistance by the North to the South, including the development of social welfare policies and programs, (e) the work for international organizations, (f) collaboration among professional social workers, to (g) the engagement in other social work activities crossing national borders.

There are a few deviating ideas on each term of the formula (multiplication) above in the title of this subsection. They remove restrictions of "categorical function" and "professional social workers" to replace them with "social work in general" and "social workers" respectively.

(ii) The incorporation of the value element (a value-focused definition and combined definition)

In the early 21st century, the factor of 'value' (purpose, aim, standard, or ethic) became a definitional element. For many authors, this value most typically meant human rights and social justice, but for others, it could mean the correction of "unidirectional" and power differentials, the achievement of an equal North-South relation, and the promotion of the social work profession, for example. Some definitions have both elements of the functional definition and the value-focused definition to become combined definitions.

(iii) The disappearance of international social work?— "Globalization"

Under globalization, 'local' social work has been globalized. Social problems on which it works, standards with which it works, and practices in which it is engaged, have been all in the globalized context. The global elements have penetrated every aspect of 'local' social work. If we suppose that international social work has been completely absorbed by it, would there still be a place for international social work to exist? If there could be, what would the relationship with 'local' social work be, and what would the roles and functions of international social work be, and what would the definition of international social work be?

(3) Some questions to come

Over Period III, some questions would come to 'the final products' and 'international social work under globalization.'

1) As soon as 'the final products' (definitions) are reported, three questions would be spontaneously raised about their content: (a) Is it appropriate for those activities/'functions' which were raised in functional definitions to be said to be those of international social work?; (b) Is it appropriate to include the 'value' elements with the specific content such as human rights which were mentioned in "value-focused definitions" and "combined definitions" under international social work?; and (c) must those activities of international social work in "functional definitions" and "combined definitions" be carried out by professional social workers?

2) The second category of questions pertains to "international social work under globalization." They are more theoretical questions on international social work. (d) The first is the question of subsection (2)(iii) just above (p.36) —if the 'local' practice is put in the global context, is the globalized 'local' practice still 'local' social work, or is it international social work? Will

international social work continue to exist? If so, what are the roles and functions of international social work while such globalized 'local' social work coexists? What will it look like? (e) How does international social work deal with the globalization of social work itself? Is it the role of international social work to globalize Western-rooted professional social work to the world? And (f) What is the contribution of international social work to the development of 'local' social work and social work itself to its third stage? (e.g. Akimoto, 2017: 1-5).

Item (a) will be answered in the next Chapter 2, and items (b) to (f) will be followed up in Chapter 3.

(4) Two additional remarks

(i) A different usage of the term 'International social work'

One is a different usage of the term 'international social work' in meaning. In some "social-work-less developed countries" such as Bhutan, Sri Lanka, and Vietnam, the term is often used to refer to the social work outside their own countries, particularly the Western-rooted professional social work of Europe, North America, Australia, New Zealand, and International social work-related organizations such as the United Nations (most typically UNICEF) and NGOs (Red Cross, Save the Children, IASSW, IFSW, etc.). 'International social work' means the social work of 'social work-developed countries,' or sometimes of any other countries including neighbouring countries.[22*] The aim of this book should allow us to put this usage aside in our following discussion.

22*   There is another usage in "less-developed countries." It could be named as international social work for schools to provide knowledge and skills to students to find and get social work jobs in other countries (cf. Vasudevan, 2003).

(ii) The review of English-medium literature mainly limited to English-speaking countries

The second remark concerns the limitation of this study which has been based on limited literature reviews. The books on which we have relied dealt with only English-medium literature, mostly from English-speaking countries. Non-English books and articles, i.e., the discussions in non-English speaking countries, even those from French, Spanish, and Portuguese speaking countries which comprise the majority worldwide,[23] have been totally or largely neglected. It is detrimental, particularly in a serious inquiry on the topic of 'what international social work is.' In addition, Russia, China, and the Middle East have been seldom discussed in the literature we reviewed.[24]

Chapter 2 is a reprint of a non-English-medium article that was written in a non-English-speaking country in the East in 1995 and explored almost the same subject in this chapter—what international social work is. In Chapters 3, the results of Chapters 1 and 2 will lead to the construction of a new definition of international social work which will hopefully be acceptable to the whole world today.

---

23   In addition to the United States, the United Kingdom, Ireland, Canada, Australia, New Zealand, and South Africa, a third of the world's countries and regions have English as their official language.

24   There may not be many publications in their languages, and if any, the content of the discussion in those non-English-speaking countries may be identical to those in English countries due to the latter's learning from the former. (cf. Ch.2 Box2-1, p.59) In that sense, the neglect may be justifiable.

References

Ahmadi. (2003). "Globalisation of consciousness and new challenges for international social work." *International Journal of Social Welfare*, 12(1): 14-23.

Akimoto, T. (1992). "Kokusaika to rōdō sōsharu wāku: Genjitsu no kokusaika, shiten no kokusaika, gainen no kokusaika" [Internationalization and Labor Social Work: Internationalization of Realities, Internationalization of 'the way of viewing matters,' and Internationalization of the Concept]." In S. Sato, (Ed.), *Kokusaika Jidai no Fukushi Kadai to Tenbō* [Welfare Issues and Perspectives in Days of Internationalization]. Tokyo: Ichiryūsha. 233-249.

Akimoto, T. (1995). "'Kokusai shakaifukushi' wo tsukuru: Kokusai Shakaifukushi no jissen/kenkyū to kijun" [To Create "the International Social Welfare/Social Work": Practice/Research of International Social Welfare/work and its Norms]. *Jurist*. Yūhikaku. 97-101.

Akimoto, T. (1997). "A voice from Japan—Requestioning International Social Work/Welfare: Where are we now? Welfare world and national interest." *Japanese Journal of Social Services*. No.1. pp.23-34. Translated and revised version of Akimoto (1995). ARIISW-Shukutoku. Gakubunsha.

Akimoto, T. (2017). "Part I: The globalization of Western-rooted professional social work and exploration of Buddhist social work. 1n Gohori, J. (Ed.), *From Western-rooted Professional Social Work to Buddhist Social Work—Exploring Buddhist Social Work.* Gakubunsha.

Akimoto, T. (2020). "Dai 1 shō: Kokusai sōsharu wōku no mokuteki to rinen" [Chapter 1: The Purpose and Idea of International Social Work]. In Oka, S. and H. Harashima (Eds.), *Sekai no Shakaifukushi 12: Kokusai Shakaifukushi* [Global Social Welfare 12: International Social Welfare]. Tokyo: Junposha. 25-50.

APASWE (Asian and Pacific Association for Social Work Education). (2013).

The Birth and Development of the APASWE—Its Forty Years of History: Rebellion, Dissemination, and Contribution. (Booklet). Asian and Pacific Association for Social Work Education.

Boehm, W. (1976). Editorial. *International Social Work.* 19(3), 1.

Cox, David, and Pawar, Manohar. (2006). *International Social Work—Issues, Strategies, and Programs.* Thousand Oaks, London and New Delhi: Sage Publications.

CSWE (Council on Social Work Education of the United States) (1956). The working committee.

Dominelli, L. (2010). *Social Work in a Globalising World.* Cambridge: Policy Press.

Falk, D. and Nagy, G. (1997). "Teaching international and cross-cultural social work." IASSW Newsletter, Issue 5.

Goldman, B.W. (1962). "International social work as a professional function. *International Social Work,* 5(3), 1-8.

Haug, E. (2005). "Critical reflections on the emerging discourse on international social work. *International Social Work,* 48(2), 126-135.

Healy, L. M. (1990). [International content in social work educational programs world-wide]. Unpublished raw data. (Cited in Healy, 2001 below.)

Healy, L. M. (1995). "Comprehensive and international overview." In T. D. Watts, D. Elliott, & N. S. Mayadas (Eds.), *International Handbook on Social Work Education.* 421-439. Westport, CT: Greenwood Press.

Healy, L. M. (2001; 2008; 2020). "What Is International Social Work?" In L. M. Healy (2001; 2008). and L. M. Healy and L. Thomas (Eds.) (2020), *International Social Work: Professional Action in an Interdependent World.* Oxford University Press, 5-13, 5-15, and 5-15 respectively.

Healy, L. M. (2012). "2 Defining International Social Work." In L. M. Healy & R. J. Link (Eds.), *Handbook of International Social Work: Human Rights, Development, and The Global Profession* (pp.9-15). New York: Oxford

University Press.

Hokenstad, M.C., Khinduka, S.K. and Midgley, J. (Eds.) (1992; 1997). *Profiles in International Social Work.* Washington, D.C.: National Association of Social Workers Press.

Huegler, Lyons, K. & Pawar, M. (2012). "1 Setting the Scene" In Lyons, K., et al. (Eds). (2012). *Handbook of International Social Work.* Sage Publications. 5-13.

Hugman, R. (2010). *Understanding International Social Work: A Critical Analysis.* Basingstoke, Hampshire: Palgrave Macmillan.

IASSW (International Association of Schools of Social Work), (1989/90)

Jebb, E. (1929). "International social service." In *International Conference of Social Work: Proceedings, Volume 1.* First Conference, Paris, July 8-13, 1928, 637-657.

Kimberly, M.D. (Ed.) (1984). *Beyond National Boundaries: Canadian Contributions to International Social Work and Social Welfare.* Ottawa: Canadian Association of Schools of Social Work.

Lavalette, M. & Ioakimdis, V. (2011). "International social work or social work internationalism? Radical social work in global perspective." In M. Lavalette (Ed.), *Radical Social Work Today: Social Work at the Crossroads.* Bristol/Portland, OR: The Policy Press. 135-52.

Lawrence, S., Lyons, K., Simpson, G. & Huegler, N. (2009). *Introducing International Social Work.* Exeter: Learning Matters.

Link, R. J. & Ramanathan, C. S. (2011). *Human Behavior in a Just World: Reaching for Common Ground.* London, MD: Rowman & Littlefield.

Lorenz, W. (1997, August). Social Work in a Changing Europe. Paper presented at the Joint European Regional Seminar of IFSW and EASSW on Culture and Identity. Dublin, Ireland, August 24, 1997.

Lyons, K. (1999). *International Social Work: Themes and Perspectives.* Aldershot: Ashgate.

Lyons, K., Manion K. & Carlsen, M. (2006). *International Perspectives on Social*

Work. Basingstoke: Palgrave Macmillan.

Lyons, K., Hokenstad, T., Pawar, M., Huegler, N. & Hall, N. (Eds.) (2012). The *SAGE Handbook of International Social Work.* Sage Publications.

Marriam-Webster. (2011).. Online dictionary London: Heinemann.

Nagy, G. & Falk, D. (2000). Dilemmas in international and cross-cultural social work education. *International Social Work,* 43(1), 49-60.

Payne, M. & Askeland, G. A. (2008). *Globalization and International Social Work: Postmodern Change and Challenge.* Aldershot, Hampshire: Ashgate.

Pawar. (2010). "Looking outwards: teaching international social work in Asia." *International Journal of Social Work Education.* 29(8), 896-909.

Sanders, D. S. & Pederson, P. (Eds.) (1984). *Education for International Social Welfare.* Manoa: University of Hawaii and Council on social Work Education.

Social Work Yearbook. Russell Sage Foundation. (Predecessor of NASW *Encyclopedia of Social Work*). Vol. 1, (1929) 229; Vol. 2, (1933) 253; Vol. 3, (1935) 214; Vol.4, (1937); Vol. 5, (1939)192.

Stein, H. (1957, January). "An international perspective in the social work curriculum." Paper presented at the Annual Program Meeting of the Council on Social Work Education, Los Angeles, January 1957.

Warren, G. (1937). "International social work." In R. Kurtz (Ed.), *Social Work Yearbook.* Vol.4. New York: Russell Sage Foundation. 224-227.

Webb, S. A. (2003). "Local orders and global chaos in social work." *European Journal of Social Work,* 6(2), 191-204.

Xu, Q. (2006). "Defining international social work: A social service agency perspective." *International Social Work,* 49(6), 679-692.

Conference, Lectures, Speeches, Presentations

Akimoto, T. 23 October 2013. "Social work education programs, professionalization and dilemmas." In the Bandung University Social Work Conference, "Strengthening the development of social work in

Indonesia." Bandung, Indonesia.

Akimoto, T. 10 November 2014. "Human resource policy framework: Is professionalization the way we take? Rejection of 'social work = professional social work." In the 17th Vietnam Social Work Day International Conference. Hanoi, Vietnam.

Akimoto, T. 23 October 2015, "Proposals to professional social work: Prepare for global crisis, rejecting IA/IF global definition. In the panel discussion, "Social work and policy in response to global crisis." APASWE/IFSW(AP) Social Work Regional Conference. Bangkok, Thailand.

Vasudevan, V. 9 February 2023. "International collaborative research project on "international social work" curricula in the Asia-Pacific region. In The 7th ARIISW-Shukutoku International Academic Forum, online, Chiba Japan.

Chapter Two

Another Understanding of International Social Work
—Not A Field of Activities but a Way of Viewing Matters—

This chapter (pp.57-87) is a translated reprint [25] of a non-English language article written in an Eastern non-English-speaking country on the same subject as one of the cited articles in Chapter 1—the exploration of what international social work is. Keeping some distance from the mainstream could lead to different views, ideas, perspectives, and a proposal of a new definition without being fully swallowed up by the mainstream. [26] The original article was written in the early 1990s.

The first section out of six presents a holistic list of activities (acts, functions, practices or research; hereinafter to be referred as 'activities') being conducted under the name of international social work. [27] The findings by Western writers in Chapter 1 were almost identical to this list. [cf. Box 2-1, p.59]

In the next section, however, the author argues that these 'activities' are not necessarily international social work, and leads us to conclude that international social work is not simply a field of 'activities' but rather 'a way of viewing matters' (perception, perspective, norms, the point of reference, approach; hereinafter to be referred as 'a way of viewing matters') at the

---

25 With revision and re-editing. See the footnote 4* on p.3 for details.

26 This piece of work does not lead to the accomplishment of the current author's ambition to understand and construct international social work acceptable to the whole world. But looking at even one country outside the English sphere would somehow contribute to this ultimate goal (cf. Ch. 1, 2.(1-2) pp.29-30).

27 The original term of "social work" in their language was *"shakaifukushi,"* which could be translated into English as "social welfare," "social policies and programs," "social work," "social development," and "(social) well-being" depending on the context. It is mostly translated as "social welfare" in the country, but in this chapter, it has been translated as "social work," neglecting the difference between these two terms.

beginning of Section 3 below. With a ten-year time-lag, in the middle of the 2000s, Western literature discussed this similar point, using the terms 'value,' 'standard' and 'purpose' (cf. Chapter 1).

The section 3 reviews the development of such background thoughts and theories to extract a core 'way of viewing matters' or the norms, such as those regarding the significance and limitation of the United Nations and its conventions; modern Western thought and fundamental human rights; the welfare state and the welfare world; the concept of a national, a world citizen, "being a human being," and an "Earthian"; the relationships of nationalism, internationalism and cosmopolitanism to each other; and a theory of the State and the nation state.

The section 4 presents a skeleton of a tentative definition of international social work, considering today's stage of development of international society. The following the section 5 measures where we are now in the course of the development of international social work in reality and in theory, and the author calls the readers' attention to the future direction of international social work.

Sections 1 and 2 answer question (a) raised in the summary section of Chapter 1 (2.(3) p.49), sections 3 and 4 to question (b) to some extent, and The section 5 would be beneficial to a discussion of question (d), although there is a difference in the core words 'internationalization' and 'globalization.'

In this article, "a non-English country" is Japan and a "non-English" language is Japanese. As far as the content is concerned, however, that discussed is not specifically about Japan but about all countries. Readers of this chapter may still find some skew towards Japan and Asia in the cited country names and cited case examples, which may be an eyesore. This happened simply because the original article was written in Japanese assuming Japanese readers. Current readers could and should replace these cited country names and case examples with the reader's own, to understand the author's real intention. The aim of this article and its reprint is to contribute to the construction of an internationally acceptable concept of international social work while utilizing the recent discussion in a specific country and in its language.

Digression for the intellectually curious

Box 2-1. Why did meanings in the Western world and in Japan tend to become identical?

While Chapter 1 reviewed literature written in English mostly in the Western world and Chapter 2 reviewed literature written in Japanese in the Far East, why is the product extracted identical? Social work is supposed to be based on the culture, tradition, and life, and political, economic, and social conditions of the society. These two societies are very different.

The reason may be because Japanese social work had simply learned and copied the Western-rooted (mainly United States') social work in content. If it is the case with other non-Western, non-English countries, the author's anxiety at the very end of Chapter 1 (2.(4)(ii) p.51)—the limitation of the literature review of the books on which we relied (while discussing 'international social work,' we have not seen other language and cultural spheres) —would be in vain, wouldn't it?

To Create 'the International Social Work'
—Practice and Research and the Way of Viewing Matters
of International Social Work[28]* —

In the past decade [the 1980s to the early 1990s], interest in international social work[29] has heightened in Japan. In the remaining years of the 20th century [sic] and in the first few decades of the 21st century, this interest will increase further. International social work seems to have been accepted as a field of social work, but what international social work actually is has not yet been agreed upon at all. This paper aims to contribute to the construction of an internationally acceptable concept of international social work through a review of recent discussions in Japan on this topic.

The article was written based on the extensive literature review of all representative books and journal articles related to international social work which was published during the 1970s to the early 1990s in Japanese in

---

28   [* indicates not original but newly-added footnotes for this reprint: hereinafter to be same.]
      * The original article is Akimoto, T. (1995b). "To create 'the international social work'—
      Practice/research and the way of viewing matters of international social work—['Kokusai-
      shakai-fukushi' wo tsukuru—Kokusai-shakaifukushi no jissen/kenkyu to kijun—],' Jurist,
      Special Issue, November 1995 (in Japanese), which was based on a presentation at the Jap-
      anese Society for Social Welfare Studies' annual conference held at Doshisha University on
      October 8, 1994. The article was translated into English and published with some revisions
      in The Journal of the Japanese Society of Social Welfare Studies. No.1, 1997. 23-34, with
      the revised title "Requestioning international social work/welfare: Where are we now?—
      Welfare world and national interest." This chapter is basically the translation of the origi-
      nal article with some revision and editing (for the publication of the above English journal
      and this book). The English is mostly based on the 1997 translated version.
29   See footnote 3.

Japan[30][31], and on some brief surveys and interviews.

1. To do What is International Social Work?
—Practice and Research Conducted Under the Name of International Social Work—

The understanding, or misunderstanding, of international social work has been confusing in various ways. What are students expecting when they register for courses named as such, and what are practitioners and researchers doing when they believe they are practicing or conducting research on international social work? The table below provides the answers obtained from the literature review and our small informal surveys and interviews. [References in Japanese on each item are mostly omitted below in this section.]

What do people call international social work? Our interest in this section is not the definition but the content or the constituent elements of what international social work is.[32] Eleven major and 18 minor concepts were identified.

Some people think that "1. studying or researching about other countries" falls into the category of international social work. This includes two sub-

---

30   Seventy-five (75) works were covered. The literature was "limited to those by the authors known as 'researchers' and practitioners in the 'social work field' and those with the term 'international social welfare/social work' or 'international welfare' as a principle." Much literature from other disciplines should have been included but has been excluded from the examination including "Development Economics, International Relations, Anthropologies, Sociology, and Psychology." Documents from the government (e.g., the Annual Report on Health and Welfare [White Paper]) and vast volumes of publications by JICA (Japanese International Cooperation Agency) must also be reviewed (Miki & Akimoto, 1998).

31   The literature review itself was made a few years earlier by the current author (T. Akimoto), but published later under a co-authorship with Miki, K. (Miki & Akimoto, 1998).

32   Re issues and problems which international social work deals with, see e.g., Figure 2 on p.301 of Kojima, 1992.

Table 2-1. Practices/Researches Conducted Under the Name of the International Social Work

1. Study/research about other countries
    a) Study/research on the social welfare situation (in general or on specific subjects) in other countries
    b) Field study/research in other countries

2. Practice of social work in other countries

3. International comparative research

4. Practice/research on issues and problems which arise in the bi-lateral or multi-lateral relationships
    a) Practice/research on issues and problems which arise at the individual level
    b) Practice/research on the effects of nature or society

5. Practice/research on issues and problems which arise on a global scale
    a) Practice/research on issues and problems which arise at the individual level
    b) Practice/research on the effects of nature or society

6. Practice/research on cross-cultural contact

7. Practice/research on "internationalisation at home"

8. "Foreign affairs" (communication; the promotion of colleagueship and friendship)

9. International exchange
    a) Friendship promotional activities
    b) Exchange of information, experience, ideas, people (students, teachers, practitioners, [and citizens]) and research
    c) Holding/participating in international conferences

10. International cooperation/collaboration
    a) Activities by the United Nations, other intergovernmental, governmental and non-governmental organisations
    b) Joint practice/research projects with practitioners, organisations or researchers in other countries

11. Practice/research on North-South relations including relief and development aid to the "Two-Thirds World"

ideas: One is "a) studying or researching the social welfare situation in other countries," such as Swedish nursing homes for the aged (sic), United States ADA (Americans with Disabilities Act), and the social welfare situation in general in various countries. (e.g., Kojima & Okada, 1994; Ogiwara, 1995) The other is "b) field research in other countries," or research conducted physically putting self in the research subject country, such as research in the slums of Dhaka or in rural villages in Peru. (Numerous examples of this 1. b), as well as ones of 2. to 5. and 10. b) below, are found in journals of various universities of social work, Japanese Society of Social Welfare Studies (1994), and many issues of International Social Work (Sage Publications).)

The simplest and most common usage of the term is to "2. practice (any) social work in other countries" than his/her own home country, not limited to "field research."

Others think that conducting "3. international comparative research" forms part of international social work. Themes could cover the whole range of social welfare policies, programs, and problems, for example, comparison among Malaysian, Indonesian, and Vietnamese child welfare, or between British and Japanese social security systems (e.g., *Encyclopaedia of Social Work* (Vol. 16 (1971) and thereafter), esp. Mohan (1987: 957-969); Furukawa (1994)).

Taking the word "international" literally, international social work should mean "4. practice or research on issues and problems which arise in a bi-lateral or multi-lateral relationship." Included are two types of practice or research on: "a) issues and problems which arise at the individual level" such as those of Japanese-Filipino children[33*] and "b) effects of nature or of society," that is, effects due to activities by a nation or some of its potent components, such as acid rain in neighbouring countries because of thermal power generation in Country A, or floods in Country B caused due to deforestation

---

33*   Children who were born in and out of wedlock between Filipino women, who worked in Japan mainly since the 1980s, and Japanese men. Many of these children had various economic, mental, and legal problems.

in an area in Country C. The cause or background of the former, a), is of course social, and the result of the latter, b), concerns individuals' lives.

Interpreting "international" as "global," international social work would be practice or research on "5. issues and problems which arise on a global scale." Poverty, the destruction of environments and ecosystems, refugees, and AIDS are examples (e.g. Kendal, 1994:11).

Some people understand cross-cultural social work and international social work to be interchangeable. "6.Practice/Research on cross-cultural contact," covers the understanding of different cultures, the conflict between them, and the efforts to solve such conflict if it occurs (cf. e.g., Sitaram, 1976). Cross-cultural counselling may be an important field within international social work practice. "Foreigners" may have many difficulties in any country.

Quite a few people turn their attention to their own countries with an "international" perspective after they have looked at other countries for a while. They question "7. internationalization at home" as being an indispensable component of international social work. In the case of Japan, some questions raised are the treatment of foreign workers, refugees, Koreans in Japan, and Japanese war orphans who returned from China.

Some people perceive the engagement in "8. foreign affairs" of organizations they belong to as being the practice of international social work. Just like the Ministry of Foreign Affairs in a state, most organizations that constitute today's society have a foreign affairs section or business with other countries. The Japan Association of Schools of Social Work [the present Japanese Association of Social Work Education], for instance, has the Special Committee of International Relations [dissolved in 2019] to contact its counterparts in other countries.

Three types of activities are included in "9. international exchange" which is executed at individual, group, organizational, and local and national government levels. The first is "a) the promotion of international friendship activities." In addition to friendship promotion at the individual level (e.g., Okada, 1985:185 emphasizes its importance), various international friendship programs have been implemented, including personnel exchange programs for members and non-members at the group and organizational levels. Being asked what sorts of international social welfare policies and programs they run, many local governments mention sister city programs, citizen exchange programs, as well as others. The second pertains to "b) exchange of information, experience, ideas, people (students, teachers, practitioners, [and citizens]) and research." The third is the "c) holding of international conferences," which is a form of b). Numerous international meetings, symposiums, and conferences have been held. They have been the central activities of international social work since the early days of its development (e.g., Each volume of *Social Work Year Book* (Russell Sage Foundation) and *Encyclopedia of Social Work* (NASW (National Association of Social Workers)); Nemoto (1989)).

Central activities of "10. international cooperation/collaboration" today are those of "a) the United Nations and other international organizations." Included are both the United Nations organizations such as ILO (International Labour Organization), WHO (World Health Organization), and UNICEF (United Nations Children's (Emergency) Fund), and voluntary international organizations such as the International Red Cross. Activities by respective states are, however, also important. Examples are ones by the United States Children's Bureau and the Japan International Cooperation Agency (JICA). Activities by NGOs (non-governmental organizations), e.g., CARE (The Cooperative for Assistance and Relief Everywhere) International and Médecins sans Frontières, have been increasing in importance recently. International social work organizations such as IASSW (International

Association of Schools of Social Work), IFSW (International Federation of Social Workers), and ICSW (International Council on Social Welfare) fall into this category. Some people understand that the engagement in "b) joint practice/research projects with practitioners, organizations or researchers of other countries" is equivalent to the practice of international social work.

Some people regard international social work as the engagement in "11. practice/research in emergency relief activities in case of wars and natural disasters and developmental assistance activities to "Two-Thirds World" with a long-term perspective. Typical activities are ones by the United Nations and other international organizations. They could be included in the sub-item "a." of "10. International cooperation and collaboration", but are put under a separate item 11. as many people associate "developing" country assistance with the term 'international social work.' John M. Romanyshyn says, "international social welfare [is] the redress of inequalities between the 'have' and 'have-not' nations." (Romanyshyn, 1971:12, cf. Ashikaga, 1985: 187) (cf. Sanders & Pedersen, 1983, cf. Okada, 1993: 16; Many publications by JICA).

The items above are not mutually exclusive. In particular, items 7. to 11. are continuous and overlapping. These items are not definitions of international social work. Each contender does not necessarily insist on any specific single item. They simply name any combination of items as international social work. For example, early versions of the *Social Work Year Book* (Russell Sage Foundation) combine "4. a) Practice/research on issues and problems which arise at the individual level," "9. c) Holding/participating in international conferences," and "10. a) Activities of the United Nations', other intergovernmental, governmental and non-governmental organizations" (e.g. Warren, 1937: 224). Recent versions of *Encyclopaedia of Social Work* add to them "3. International comparative research," "9. a) Friendship promotion activities," "11. Aid to developing countries," and others (e.g. NASW, 18th ed., 1987). Y. Kojima and L. Healy (1993) include "3. International comparative research," "5. Practice/research on issues and problems which arise on the global scale," "9. a) Friendship promotion activities," "6. Practice/ research concerning cross-cultural contact," and others (cf. e.g., Tani, 1993: 54).

2. This Is Not Necessarily International Social Work

Scanning the list above, it seems as if anything that concerns "other countries" is considered international social work. The author's understanding is different. It might not be international social work to carry out any one item in the list or a combination of several items. Why is this not necessarily international social work? There are two reasons: Firstly, simple and plain questions arise on each item, and secondly historical development should not be neglected. We will discuss the first point in this section, and the second point in the next section.

Simple and plain questions arise on each activity item in the list. Here we cannot describe all items in detail, but in a word, it is not necessarily international social work if we do something related to foreign countries. Let's cover the points on our list in Table 2-1 above.

Firstly, to "study/research other countries" (1.) or "the social welfare problem and situation (in general or on a specific topic) of other countries" (1. a)) is not necessarily international social work. To study and describe the history or the present state of social welfare in other countries would be something that could be called "overseas information" or "the situation abroad." Once we start this kind of thing, it becomes endless.

Studying Swedish nursing homes, the United States' ADA (Age Discrimination Act), child labour in Bolivia and Bangkok urban slums might not be international social work. They may be part of domestic social work. Because of the internationalization of society, each field of social work, such as social work for the aged, people with disabilities, children, and the poor, could not be completed unless it deals with issues and problems beyond its national boundary.

To conduct a "Field study/research in other countries" (1. b) may not be necessarily international social work (Akimoto, 1995a). "Field research" here means the research that is conducted in the field or country of the research subjects. The meaning is broader than the "field research" in typical useage. Isn't it strange to say that to do a certain thing in a foreign country is international social work and to do the same thing in his/her own country is not international social work but domestic ('local' in Chapter 1; 'national' in Chapter 3) social work? Just imagine two cases in which a Japanese researcher analysed of poverty of London in London and then did the same in Tokyo.

Students and professors from China and Korea do research on the problems of Japanese elderly people and give presentations in Japanese academic societies' annual conferences—it is international social work, and is it domestic social work if Japanese practitioners and researchers do the same?

Nothing would be different if you draw some lessons for your own country in 1. a) and b) and in other activities in the following items. It is domestic social work if you draw a lesson for your own country, isn't it?

Replacing the "field research" (1.b)) with "practice", are whatever "practices social workers do in other countries" (2.) international social work? If a United States Christian NGO's work in a Calcutta [Kolkata] slum should be called an international social work practice, why not an Indian nun's work in a Chicago slum soup kitchen? (Physician Task Force, 1985) Do United States professional social workers accept this as an international social work? The engagement in practice in "developing countries" is international social work, isn't it? (e.g., Brown & Pizer, 1987) More seriously—if Japanese social workers' practice in Asian countries could be called international social work, should Japanese researchers' work in the South Manchuria Railway

Company Research Department before World War Two and the practitioners' work to transfer Japanese social work to "Manchuria" and the Korean Peninsula be so called? (cf. e.g., Shen, 1995) Is it called international social work if a social worker from the United Kingdom comes to an Asian country and designs a social welfare program, trains social workers for the operation or repeats casework in communities administer the colonized country smoothly? Suzerain states in the northern hemisphere did much in such countries. Can what they did be termed international social work?

In more basic terms, this approach argues that a Japanese person doing something in Japan corresponds to domestic social work practice, but a Kenyan or an Australian doing the same in Japan constitutes international social work practice (and vice versa). This does not seem very rational.

"International comparative research" (3.) and analysis are just some of the most primitive research methods that are nothing special to social work but are common to all disciplines, fields, and themes. This has always been the case.

"Practice/research on cross-cultural contact" (6.) is not equal to international social work. Cross-cultural and multi-cultural social work is important even in international social work but has nothing to do with only the relations between countries. It is important also within a country. We could not call it international social work.[34*]

"Practice/research on internationalization at home" (7.), in the social worker's own countries, may or may not be international social work. It is not

---

34*　In a forum in Tokyo in January 2018 where the Presidents of the IASSW and APASWE (Asian and Pacific Association for Social Work Education) as well as Prof. Lynne Healey (cf. Chapter 1) attended, the presenters and participants all agreed on this understanding (Matsuo, Akimoto, and Hattori, 2019: 76). The forum was organized by the Asian Research Institute for International Social Work (ARIISW), Shukutoku University, cosponsored by IASSW, APASWE, and the Japanese Association for Social Work Education. It was supported by the Japanese Society for the Study of Social Welfare, the Japanese Society for the Study of Social Work, and the Japanese Society for the Study of Social Work Education.

easy to call activities international social work when the activities discourage the intake of refugees or encourage migrant workers to be assimilated into Japanese culture and society.

Accepting visitors from other countries, exchanging MOUs (Memorandum of Understandings) with universities of other countries, and being engaged in exchange programs with students, teachers, and researchers (cf. 9. b)), and devoting efforts to the international relations committee of national associations of social work (cf. 10. a)) would not necessarily be called international social work, although they contribute to communication, the promotion of colleagueship, and friendship. Shouldn't these activities be called diplomacy or "foreign affairs" (8.) which are commonly practiced day by day by almost all organizations in today's society including private corporations?

Is it international social work to attend and make a research presentation at a conference (9. c)) which an international social work organization organises, or to be invited by another country and make a keynote speech at an international conference?

Is it an international social work practice to work for a United Nations agency, an NGO, or such a hard-core international social work organizations (10. a)) as the IASSW, IFSW, or ICSW?

Executing joint research projects with researchers from other countries ((10. b)) would not necessarily be international social work (Akimoto, 1995a). In a Japan-United States joint research project, is it international social work for a Japanese researcher but just social work for a US researcher to do research on poverty in a big United States city? Suppose a joint research team on problems of Japanese elderly people was formed, is it international social work for Chinese or Korean team members and also for Japanese members, or is it domestic social work for the Japanese members?

The discussion on South-North relationships (11.) would not necessarily be international social work. Are the practice and research of aid activities carried out to expand the market of his/her own country and promote the national interest of his/her own country international social work? Aren't they domestic social work? It is not easy to affirm that the engagement in ODA (Official Development Assistance) projects is international social work.

3. What is International Social Work?

Practice and research under each item in the above list may or may not be called international social work. So, what is international social work? International social work is not a category of activities but rather 'a way of viewing matters' (norms; approach), (Akimoto, 1995a; International social work may be called a branch in this meaning).

This leads to the question of what is 'the way of viewing matters'? The same literature review as that in the section 1 above identified two streams: (1) NASW's *Encyclopaedia of Social Work*[35]—W. A. Friedlander[36]—Y. Kojima and (2) G. Myrdal and R. Pinker—Y. Ashikaga and T. Okada.

(1) Viewed from the outside

Y. Kojima (1992) writes the following paragraphs:

Even if the legislation and the administration and voluntary welfare services are not yet well prepared in a country…the position of international social work is to examine its imperfection, to develop welfare services for the socially disadvantaged and their families, and to clear frontiers of new practice (p.288).

---

35 Each edition of Social Work Year Book and Encyclopedia of Social Work, esp. 13th ed. (1957) of the latter.

36 Friedlander, 1961 and 1975.

At the United Nations level, without defining social welfare narrowly, they discuss the guarantee of human rights of women, children, the disabled, the aged, refugees, minorities, migrant workers and others, and criticize and attack mercilessly other countries when their rights are disturbed in other countries or by their own establishment so that the social justice is advanced. Through the process...representatives of United Nations membership countries join their hands to draft resolutions and declarations, to contribute to the advancement of policies on human rights of each country, spending many years, and to make efforts to be concluded into effective conventions and protocols, if an agreement that it is necessary to do so is reached among countries (p.288).

Fundamental human rights have been guaranteed by a state's constitution and laws. What it means is that people can insist on their rights and seek relief based on laws within the extent and limit they provide for, when those rights are encroached. However, if the extent of laws is made limited and changed for the worse, they lose the base of the complaint, and cannot help give in to their fate. Because the guarantee of human rights is under its state's authority, other countries cannot only criticize a country's infringement of foreigners' human rights, which are out of the protection of laws, but are rather criticized as "domestic interference" by the country concerned. Meanwhile, traditionally domestic laws have been stipulated with the idea that "individuals belong to a state," but if the state ratifies the International Convention on Human Rights, and its treaty powers which guarantee individuals' rights, do not rely on the state any more... International legislation makes "people who obey the state" able to live in "a state which exists for individuals" (pp.289-290).

[English translation by TA]

The significance of Kojima is her understanding of social work from outside the state. On the other hand, she discusses only the level of positive law, placing too high a value on the United Nations, and relies too much on the International Declaration of Human Rights and the International Convention on Human Rights.

(2) Beyond the Welfare State to a Welfare World

Y. Ashikaga (1985) and T. Okada (1985) cite G. Myrdal and R. Pinker respectively to write the following paragraphs respectively:

"The fact is that the setting in which the modern Welfare State has been developing in the Western world has been one of progressive international disintegration. It is equally undeniable that the larger part of the complex system of public policies in the interest of national progress, and of the growth of equality and security for the individual, which today make up the Welfare State, have on balance tended to disturb the international equilibrium. They were nowhere conceived and brought into effect as internationally concerted actions. Effects abroad were not taken into consideration." (Myrdal, 1960:160-161)* In that sense, the modern welfare state is nationalistic. "[T]he strengthening of the ties within the individual nations and the increasing scope of national economic planning have tended to push towards international disintegration" (Myrdal, 1960:285)*. Thus, the conclusion of the ultimate solution is "…there is no alternative to international disintegration except to begin, by international cooperation and mutual accommodation, to build the Welfare World" (Myrdal, 1960:176)* (Ashikaga, p.187).

[*Myrdal's citation was added by the current author.]

The idea of the "welfare world," which can be obtained by extending the concept of the "welfare state" guarantees the human minimum, rather than national minimum, as a right that derives simply from being a member of human society, and requires world society to fulfil this duty...It is the internationalism of the social welfare that the "welfare state" ought to be extended to a "welfare world," putting the conceptual base of social welfare on the human rights and unlimited altruism. In reality, however, it has been blocked by a thick wall of nationalism. For, as R. Pinker (1979) points out...in his *The Idea of Welfare*, social welfare has an aspect to maintain boundaries and has been confined within an institution of a state because of its national egoism. A state is not only a container but also a wall. Nationalism is necessary but must be open-ended. Internationalism and nationalism are thus two moments that exist within (Okada, p.185).

[English translation by TA]

The significance of the above quotes is their concern for the underlying thought. They question the historical meaning and limitation of the welfare state, insert it as a "parameter", and envisage a welfare world beyond it. They let us extract a national boundary, a wall of social welfare, as a central element of international social work.

Digression for the intellectually curious

Box 2-2. Why did meanings in the Western world and in Japan became different?

While Chapters 1 and 2 reviewed literature discussing the same subject, "What is international social work?" based on Western-rooted professional social work, why did only Chapter 2 review literature with an interest in the background thought and theories, such as the welfare world, which were still Western-rooted?

The reason may be the language issue. Both use different languages. One is English, the other is Japanese. The English term "social work" has been often translated into "shakaifukushi" in Japanese, which may cover not only social work in the Western sense but also social welfare, social policy, social development, and social wellbeing as well. Naturally a conceptual discrepancy is born in the coverage and meaning. Due to this "misunderstanding" (judging from the original English social work world's point of view), the unexpected conceptual development of social work could be possible insofar as we consider social work on a world scale.

4. Not to See and Think from the Perspective of One's Own Country
—A tentative definition and 'the way of viewing matters' of international social work—

The following is a tentative definition at the most abstract level of international social work with learning from these two streams above and with consideration of the present developmental stage of the world, which will be discussed in the following subsections 5.(1) and (2) on pp.78-81:

International social work is to think about the welfare of international society (all people in the world) and to make efforts to realize it. The key concept is "judgement from the outside." 'The way of viewing matters' with which we think and make efforts is what exists outside their own country and is commonly usable in the international society.[37]

The prime theme in international social work would be 1) What is 'the way of viewing matters'? 2) Is it possible to form and materialize this international 'way of viewing matters' in today's reality of nation states as the mainstream, and if possible, how? and 3) How are people who think and work with such a 'way of viewing matters' born? Here we touch on 1) and 2) In Chapter 4 we consider 3).

1) What is 'the way of viewing matters'? It is something on the opposite pole of nationalism and national interest. It is the claim from thinking of a welfare world, a citizen of the world, and "as a human being."[38] (Akimoto, 1995a) 'The way of viewing matters' is not only those of the International Declaration of Human Rights and the International Convention on Human Rights. "Positive laws" agreed by each state in the United Nations are easiest to accept as 'the way of viewing matters,' but there would be others. Contrarily, some activities of the United Nations may not be usable as 'the way of viewing matters' of international social work.[39] NGOs are sometimes different from and conflict with them in opinion. 'The way of viewing matters' here is that social norm in international society. The key is to find what the norms are and formulate them.

---

37 'The way of viewing matters' may be incorporated into their own country's 'way of viewing matters.'

38 Many NGOs and social work-related people have a liking for these terms to use.

39 The United Nations is meaningful and crucially important, but more sociological analyses are necessary. It should not be forgotten that it is the stage of conflicts of each country's national interests.

2) Is such 'a way of viewing matters' possible? In the reality of the nation-state world, is it possible to force the concession to nationalism and national interest for the welfare world, a citizen of the world, a cosmopolitan, and "as a human being"? Is a welfare world realistic, as well as these other concepts, which are seemingly super-historical and are frequently found in both the mass media and NGO and academic literature recently, theoretically and practically?

Theoretically, we have learned the limitations of welfare states. Philosophically, we have had the ideas of the Western Enlightenment finding their way to the International Declaration of Human Rights. Some articles of a nation-state's (e.g. Japanese) Constitution and some laws such as the Labour Standards Act, do not distinguish between its own nationals and non-nationals. Some religions have for a long time preached the equality and brotherhood of people before God. There could be other forms of progress.

5. Where Are We Now?[40]

One difficulty is in measuring how far an actual society has already prepared for such 'a way of viewing matters' or norms.

(1) In an actual society: Solid nation states and national boundaries

Today in reality, national boundaries have also been lowered.[41] For example, a woman who was born in France, moved immediately to Nigeria, received a higher education in the United States, married a Mexican, and is now working in Singapore. She loves all those countries and has difficulty describing her nationality. Needless to say, the numbers of migrants, foreign workers, and refugees are increasing.

There exist numerous associations in the sociological sense, both multi-national corporations (Okada, 1985; 185) and non-profit international organizations, which span national boundaries. There is not only the United Nations but also the EU (European Union), ASEAN (Association of South-East Asian Nations), NAFTA (North American Free Trade Agreement) [ineffective in 2020], etc. The NAALC (North American Agreement on Labor Cooperation), the labour side of NAFTA, stipulates that cases of violation or unsatisfactory implementation of labour laws in a party country go to a review board (National Administration Office) in other party countries. Most discussions and agreements at G7 meetings would have been shouted down as "domestic interference" a few decades ago.

Mutual dependency or the effect of a country's economy on other countries has been dramatically increasing. The world has reached the point

---

40 Subsections (1) and (2) of this Section 5 are from Akimoto, 1997: 28-29 and 29-30 respectively.

41 We have entered not an era of exploring ideas but an era of empirically measuring where we are now heading toward the welfare world, and how much society has prepared for it.

where economic superpowers cannot even protect their national interests if they think only of their own interest. (Kagami, 1995; Akimoto, 1992; 243) Information encircles the globe in an instant as if there were no national boundaries. The existence of nuclear weapons and the problem of the Earth's ecosystem make national boundaries meaningless. (Ashikaga, 1985: 188)

Contrarily, nation states certainly exist and their reality is conflicting national interests. Just remember the simple fact that we still cannot cross national borders without passports which say, for instance, "The Minister for Foreign Affairs of [Country A] requests all those whom it may concern to allow the bearer, a [Country A's] national, to pass freely and without hindrance and in case of need, to afford him or her every possible aid and protection" even though the bearer may not have asked for the patronage of the state[42*] Even the United Nations is an aggregation of nation states. The agreements and operations of the above organizations abbreviated (p.78) are also compromised by competing national interests.

Can NGOs with some social cause such as environment protection or "being a woman" surpass national borders? These are the kinds of questions we hear about of late. Even being a class does not surpass national borders. The international solidarity of the labour movement across national boundaries has not yet been successfully achieved. More fundamentally speaking, social welfare today has been designed or is even often defined as the rights of the people from a state or obligations/services of a state to the people. Is it possible to see a human being before his or her nationality?

42*   Many European people spontaneously refer to EU and Shengen Agreement areas and insist on the change of the meaning of national boundaries, but we will not get in this subject here. Seeing from the whole world, these areas (countries) share just small parts, and the change pertains to the relation only among those countries and the "national boundaries" between those member countries and non-member countries have firmly existed.

(2) In theory: Not a welfare world but internationalized states

While national boundaries have been disappearing much on one side, nation states have firmly continued to exist. In such a setting we need to examine the following questions. What is a welfare world? How will it be achieved? Where are we now on our way to a welfare world?[43*] Here we discuss only the third question.[44]

Today is said to be an age when we are required to be good citizens of a nation, good international citizens, and good world citizens all at the same time. A state and its social welfare could be thought of in this analogy. We are requested to be a good nation state providing good domestic social welfare, to be a good internationalized state with good internationalized social welfare, and to have a perspective on a welfare world[45] and world welfare, at the same time.

The importance here is the second term, that is, an internationalized state and its internationalized social welfare. Because of internationalization or even globalization,[46] a state and its social welfare must be internationalized.

Internationalization implies triple points of discussion. Firstly, the basic nature is still national although the period for the judgment on the national interest might be longer than in the first term, that is, a state and its domestic social welfare. In this sense, a welfare world and world welfare will not necessarily arise as an extension of the internationalization of each state and its social welfare.

43* Many European people spontaneously refer to EU and Shengen Agreement areas and insist on the change of the meaning of national boundaries, but we will not get in this subject here. Seeing from the whole world, these areas (countries) share just small parts, and the change pertains to the relation only among those countries and the "national boundaries" between those member countries and non-member countries have firmly existed.

44 Strictly speaking, to discuss the latter without discussing the former two is irrational.

45 The relation between a welfare world and the world state has not been fully discussed yet.

46 The difference and relation between internationalization and globalization are not referred to here.

Secondly, internationalization requires the erasure of national boundaries to some extent. It does not deny a state as a policy subject but refuses to attach a special meaning or importance to a specific state. For example, we do not think that Japan is a special state. We start from the point that Japan is a state which is just the same as other states. It does not start from the perspective of the Japanese, but from one of all peoples. Furthermore, it often leads us to start not as a Japanese but as a human being or an individual. In a way, it requires us to be cosmopolitan before being international. (Akimoto, 1992:243) In other words, international social work contains within it a path to a welfare world. Is the development from within (or the denial of self) possible? If possible, how?

Thirdly, "internationalization" can be used to describe various activities in the process of a state's more abrupt economic, social, and cultural expansion. Sometimes the word is a euphemism for imperialistic invasion. The internationalization of the economy is the independent variable and the internationalization of social work is the dependent variable. The timing coincides perfectly with the appropriate time lag. Even a developmental project can be for poverty alleviation or for a "developed" country's economic expansion. More difficult is that a project carries both aspects at the same time.

(3) The location of your country

[The following is the case of Japan. Each reader is expected to rewrite the content of this subsection replacing "Japan" with his/her own country.] (The insertion for this book publication.)

We need to exercise caution with Japanese discussion on international social work. (1) Almost all Japanese respondents and writers in our surveys, interviews, and literature reviews created the preceding list of items perceived only from a Japanese viewpoint, and only in relation to Japan and the internationalization of Japanese social work. Most of them were busy asking about the role of Japan and Japanese contribution, or the doctrine of atonement. They never leave behind their nationality. (2) The period when discussion on international social work in Japan grew is suggestive. It was from the latter half of the 80s, which coincided with the expansion of the Japanese economy into other countries, especially Asia.

The essence of international social work is 'the way of viewing matters' of the international society, that is, not from national interests.[47]

6. Summary

People have conducted various activities and given them the name of international social work as practice and research on and in other countries; on issues and problems which arise in the bi-lateral or multi-lateral relationships or on a global scale; on the North-South relations; on cross-cultural contact; about "internationalization at home" as well as international comparative research; "foreign affairs"; international exchange; and international cooperation/collaboration.

However, to do these activities is not necessarily international social work. All that concerns other countries do not come under the concept of international social work. They may or may not be. International social work should be defined not as a category of activities but rather as 'a way of viewing matters,' or efforts towards the welfare world envisaged beyond

---

47   Some people may argue that today in a shorter term in human history, the surging mass unemployment and nationalism in "developed" countries is a more central subject for international social work.

welfare states.

Today is a time when to be a nation state, to be internationalized, and to have a perspective for a welfare world are required at the same time. With this recognition, we won't miss key elements of international social work today, that is, national boundaries, national interests, and nationalism, as well as a dream for the welfare world. Practice/research and chattering with the lack of recognition of where we are now are not only useless but are also hazardous. International social work is a challenging topic but at the same time a risky one.

International social work is redefined as efforts of the international society whose 'way of viewing matters,' or norms, are ones not from your own countries as to fit today's developmental stage of the society. International social work implies an orientation against national interests and nationalism.

References

Akimoto, T. (1992). "Kokusaika to rōdō sōsharu wāku: Genjitsu no kokusaika, shiten no kokusaika, gainen no kokusaika" [Internationalization and Labor Social Work: Internationalization of Realities, Internationalization of 'the way of viewing natters,' and Internationalization of the Concept]." In S. Sato, (Ed.), *Kokusaika Jidai no Fukushi Kadai to Tenbō* [Welfare Issues and Perspectives in Days of Internationalization]. Tokyo: Ichiryūsha. 233-249.

Akimoto, T. (1995a). "Shakaifukushi ni okeru kokusaika: Kokusaika to nashonarizumu" [Internationalization of Social Welfare: Internationalization and Nationalism]. In Ichibangase, Y. (Ed.). *Nijū-isseiki Shakaifukushi-gaku* [The 21 Century Social Welfare]. Tokyo: Yū hikaku. 156-169.

Akimoto, T. (1995b). "Kokusai-shakaifukushi' wo tsukuru: Kokusai-shakaifukushi no jissen/kenkyū to kijun" [To Create 'the International Social Work': Practice/research and 'the way of viewing matters' of International Social Work],' *Jurist*, Special Issue, November 1995 Yū hikaku (in Japanese), which was based on a presentation at the Japanese Society for Social Welfare Studies' annual conference held at Doshisha University on October 8, 1994.

Akimoto, T. (1997). "Requestioning international social work/welfare: Where are we now? —Welfare: world and national interest." *The Journal of the Japanese Society of Social Welfare Studies*. No.1, 1997. 23-34. The English translation of Akimoto, 1995b with some revisions and the revised title.

Ashikaga, Y. (Autumn, 1985). "Kokusai-shakaifukushi josetsu" [Introduction to International Social Welfare]. *Social Work Research* [*Sōsharu Wāku Kenkyu*], Vol.11, No.3.

Brown, J. L. & Pizer, H. F. (1987). *Living Hungry in America*. Macmillan. Translation: Aoki. K. (1990). *Gendai Amerika no Kiga* [Hunger in the Present United States]. (Nan'un-dō).

Encyclopedia of Social Work. (NASW). Each edition.

Fasteam, I. J. (1957). "International Social Welfare". *Encyclopedia of Social Work. 13th ed*. NASW.

Freidlander, W. A. (1961). *Introduction to Social Welfare*, 2nd ed. Englewood Cliffs, NJ: Prantice Hall.

Furukawa, K. (1994). "Kokusaika-jidai no shakaifukushi to sono kadai: Hikaku shakaifukushi no kisoteki shomonndai wo chushin ni"[Social Welfare in the Days of Internationalization and its Challenges: Focusing on Basic Issues of Comparative Social Welfare] *Social Welfare* [Shakaifukushi-gaku] (Japanese Society for Social Welfare Studies) Vol.35 No.1 (the 50th volume of the set).

Hagiwara, Y. (1995). "Ajia no shakaifukushi" [Social Welfare in Asia] Chuō Hōki Shuppan.

International Social Work. Sage Publications.

Japanese Society for Social Welfare Studies (1994). *Shakaifukushi ni okeru Kokusai-kyōryoku no Arikata ni kansuru Kenkyū* [Research on International Collaboration in Social Welfare] (basic research). Japanese Society for Social Welfare Studies.

Kagami, M. (1995). *Hitobito no Ajia Nakamura Shōji-cho (Shohyū)* [Asia of People by Shōji Nakamura (book review)] *Asahi Shimbun*. Jan. 15 Morning edition.

Kendal, K. A. (1993) "Sōgo ni izon shiau sekai no naka no shakaifukushi" [Interdependent Social Work in the World], *Shakaifukushi Kyōiku Nenpō* [Social Work Education Annual Report] (Japanese Association of Schools of Social Work) Vol.14.

Kojima, Y. (1992). "Kokusai-shakaifukushi Kakuritsu no Kiban" [The Foundation of the Establishment of International Social Work"]. In Sato S. (Ed.). *Kokusaikajidai no Fukushi-kadai to Tenbo* [Welfare Issues and Perspectives in the Era of Internationalization]. Tokyo: Ichiryūsha. 278-303.

Kojima, Y. & Okada, T (Eds.) (1994). *Sekai no Shakaifukushi* [Social Work in the World]. Gakuensha.

Kojima, Y. & Healy, L. (1993). "A Comparative Research on International Social Work Research in Japan and the United States." *Shakaifukushi Kyōiku Nenpō* [Social Welfare Education Annual Report]. Vol.14.

*Matsuo, K., Akimoto, T. and Hattori, M. (2019). *What Should Curriculums for International Social Work Education Be?* (The 3rd Shukutoku University International Forum; 20 January 2019). Asian Research Institute for International Social Work (ARIISW), Shukutoku University, Japanese Association for Social Work Education (JASWE), and Japanese Society for the Study of Social Work (JSSSW).

Miki, K. and Akimoto, T. (1998). "Bunken wo tōshite mita nihon no 'Kokusai-shakaifukushi' Kenkyu " [Literature Review: 'International Social Work' in Japan]. *Social Welfare* (Social Welfare Department of

Japan Women's University). 31-42.

Mohan, B. (1987). 'International Social Welfare·Comparative Systems.' *Encyclopedia of Social Work*. NASW, Silver Spring, MD. 18th ed. 957-969.

Myrdal, G. (1960). *Beyond the Welfare State*. New Haven and London: Yale University Press. Supervising translation: Kitagawa, K. (1963) *Fukushikokka wo koete* [Beyond the Welfare State] Diamond Sha.

Nemoto, Y. (1989). "Kokusai shakaifukushi no enkaku" [A History of International Social Welfare] In Nakamura, Y. et al. (Eds.) *Shakaifukushi Kyōshitsu* [Social Welfare Class] (enlarged, revised edition) Yūhikaku.

Okada, T. (Totaro) (Autumn 1985). "Kantōgen" [Foreword]. *Sosharu waku Kenkyu* [Social Work Research] Vol.11, No.3. 185.

Okada, T.(Toru) (1993). *Shakaifukushi Kyōiku Nenpō* [Social Work Education Annual Report] (Japanese Association of Schools of Social Work) Vol.14.

Physician Task Force on Hunger in America. (1985). *Hunger in America: The Growing Epidemic*. Middletown: CN, Wesleyan University Press.

Pinker, R. (1979). *The Idea of Welfare*. London: Heinemann Educational. Translation: Hoshino, M. & Ushikubo, N. (2003) *Shakaifukushi: Mittsu no Moderu* [Social Welfare: Three Models] Reimei-shobo.

Romanyshyn, J. M. (1971). *Social Welfare; Charity to Justice*. Random House.

Sanders, D. S. & Pedersen, P. ed., (1983) *Education for International Social Welfare* (Hawaii: CSWE/University Hawaii School of Social Work).

Shen, J. (1995) *Manshūkoku ni okeru Shakaijigyō no Tenkai* [Evolution of Social Work in "Manchukuo"] (Dissertation).

Sitaram, K. S. (1976). *Foundation of Intercultural Communication*. (Carbondale, IL: Southern Illinois University). Translation: Midooka, K. (1985) *Ibunka Komyunikeshon—Ōbei-chūshin-shugi kara-no Dakkyaku—* [Cross-cultural Communication] Tokyo Sōgensha.

Social Work Year Book. (New York: Russell Sage Foundation). Each edition.

Tani, K. (1993). "Kokusai fukushi kyoiku no kadai" [Tasks of International Welfare Education] *Shakaifukushi Kyōiku Nenpō* [Social Welfare Education

Annual Report] Vol.14.

Warren, G. L. (1937). "International Social Work". Russell H. Kurtz (Ed.). *Social Work Year Book. 4th Issue.* New York: Russell Sage Foundation.

Chapter Three

A New Construction of International Social Work

Chapter 3 approaches a new understanding of the term 'international social work' and sets out a proposal for a new construction of international social work itself, being based on the results in Chapters 1 and 2, and taking lessons from them.

This chapter begins by taking two of the models of the conceptual development of international social work from Chapters 1 and 2 respectively. They are models, so do not necessarily coincide with chronological historical actualities in content. Between the two models, there are five major differences.

These differences are as follows: 1. The inductive construction from the review of actual history vs. the deductive construction from 'the theory of the State'; 2. dealing with the phase when there were practices which were same as or similar to those under international social work in its later phases but having no names or terms as such, as 'pre-history' or as a part of the history of international social work; 3. the focus on 'value' vs. on 'the way of viewing matters'; 4. the understanding of social work (or the distinction between social work and social workers, and between people who do social work and "social workers" who do social work as a gainful occupation; and 5. the dissemination of the existing mainstream social work through globalization vs. the new construction of international social work from zero or based on and comprehending various 'indigenous' 'social work' among all people, localities, countries and all kinds of social work, which may not have the name and concept of 'social work.' While learning from the models, a brief tentative response to the questions raised at the end of Chapter 1 will be provided.

After these 'warming-up exercises,' this chapter will proceed to the new construction of international social work. The following steps will be taken: The examination of the meaning of "international," nations and national borders, the specification of the purpose and the target population for whom international social work works, and the identification of 'the way of viewing matters' (cf. 'value' in Chapter 1; 'norm' as used in Chapter 2) to be incorporated, and international social work's relationship with globalized 'national' ('local' in the words of Chapter 1; hereinafter to be referred as 'national' in this chapter) social work and with the development of social work itself to the next stage. The summary and conclusion will be shown in the form of a new definition, which connotes the elements above. Lastly, for new visitors to this subject, an overview of the newly constructed International Social Work will be made, being unafraid of duplication.

1. Two Models of Conceptual Development of International Social Work and Questions on the Achievement of International Social Work of Western-rooted (Professional) Social Work
(Follow-up of Chapters 1 and 2)

1.1 Simplified Models of the Conceptual Development of International Social Work

Figure 3-1 represents the simplified models of the conceptual development of international social work, one developed from the summary table (Table 1-1) of the mainstream (Western-rooted professional) social work in Chapter 1 with some help from the findings of Chapter 2, and the other developed from the interpretation and lessons of Chapter 2.

Figure 3-1. Simplified models of the development of the concept of Inter-

Phase	'A Theory of the State'
I The Birth of ISW No words, no concepts	The birth of nation states and national borders **'Mainstream' Model** (Prehistory) (Chapter 1 origin)
II The Birth of the Term and its Growth **"International"** **social work** (Social work related to "international")	**(Period I) → (Period II)** <Social work related to other countries and beyond, crossing and concerning national borders> (by social workers)
III The Maturity of the Concept **"International** **social work"** (An independent concept) Exploration of the concept-"What is ISW?" Definitions (The final product)	**(Period II) → (Period III)** <Certain categories of social work activities/functions> 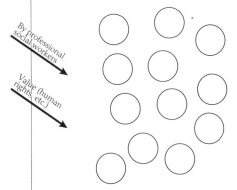 <Certain categories of social work activities/functions with certain values> (human rights, social justice, democracy, the promotion of the profession, etc.), performed by professional social workers.
IV Re-examination under Internationalization/ Globalization and the future of ISW For the population of the whole world	**(Period III)** The globalization of problems, standards & practices ISW will disappear or expand. Globalization (dissemination) of existing Western-rooted professional sosial work with or without indigenization A global profession

< >: definitional understandings in respective Phase/Period

<SW & Nations>

del (Chapter 2 origin)	
Social work related to other countries and beyond, crossing and oncerning national borders> irtual ISW activities following the nomenclature in the later hases	Social work National borders (ISW) SW Development of social work
→ are not necessarily ISW.	SW transferred to and embraced by a state

he second birth of ISW, being outside of the state sovereignty
 	
Social work activities with the certain 'way of viewing matters'>
  Viewed by eyes from the outside;
  Compound Eyes;
  Eyes beyond/from the outside of nation states; from the world
 	
  Reemphasis of the constituency of all people on the earth;
  'The way of viewing matters' which puts no special significance
n any specific countries and regions including one's own.)
 	
Social work with a certain way of viewing matters>
erformed by anyone, to promote of the wellbeing of all people
n the earth. No special significance of any specific countries
nd regions including one's own.
	The limit of nation states= welfare states
	
	Spinning out of the sovereignty of states
	
	ISW NSW
	
	Beings or organizations out of nation states e.g. UN, INGOs

W continues as long as nation states and national borders continue o exist. onstruction of ISW based on and subsuming various social works from zero to an ISW to be applicable for all people, countries and ocial works) evelopment of social work to the next stage	(The world federation of nations) (Welfare world)

SW: Social work
NSW: 'National' social work
ISW: International Social Work

The development of the concept of international social work is divided into four phases in the first column. The phases are as follows:

◆ Phase I: The birth of international social work

This is the phase in which there are "No words, no concepts," but there is virtual (identical) international social work following the nomenclature in the later phases.

◆ Phase II: The birth of the term '"international social work"' and its growth

This is the phase of "International" social work. All social work related to 'international' is named international social work.

◆ Phase III: Maturity of the concept

"International" social work in Phase II turns into the term 'international social work,' and the exploration of the concept, "What is international social work?" is pursued to its final definitions.

◆ Phase IV: Reexamination under internationalization/globalization and the future

This is the phase of self-conflict and reexamination to make international social work that of the population of the whole world, partly related to globalization.

(1) Mainstream model, Chapter 1-origin

The second column of Figure 3-1 shows the mainstream model converted from Chapter 1, Table 1-1, with some help from the fruits of Chapter 2. It begins with the first use of the term 'international social work,' and the whole development is divided into three phases (Periods) instead of the four of the first column above. Phase I of "No name, no concept" is missing and treated as "Prehistory."

Period I of the model (Phase II in the first column of Figure 3-1) represents years of "international" social work. All social work 'activities' that are related to other countries or beyond, crossing and concerning national borders are regarded as international social work. In the actual history of mainstream international social work, Jebbs' presentation at the 1928 international social work conference was the first example of its use. It referred to the activities of international organizations such as the Red Cross and Save the Children and the need for joint research work, under the name of international social work. Warren was the first to write an article dealing with this, titled, "International Social Work" in the 1937 *Social Work Yearbook*.

Period II of the model (Phase III in the first column) is the period when the concept of 'international social work' —what international social work is—is explored. Certain categories of 'activities' (acts or 'functions' as it is referred to in some parts of Chapter 1) are named as such among all social work activities that are related to other countries or beyond, crossing and concerning national borders. In mainstream history, even Warren in the previous period identified activities exceeding national borders to serve for domestic case work (e.g., immigrants), practices in countries outside of the social workers' home countries, aid and assistance to war and disaster victims and depressed people in other countries, and working in international organizations. In addition, through this phase, exchange (of information, knowledge, opinions, ideas, experiences, and colleagueship through conferences, mutual visits, and joint research), comparative research, cross cultural practices as well as other international-related activities were also counted as international social work. In the process, two key elements—"by professional social workers" and "value" (e.g., human rights, social justice, the promotion of professional

Figure 3-2.
The mainstream model definition

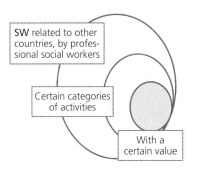

SW related to other countries, by professional social workers

Certain categories of activities

With a certain value

SW: Social work

social work, and democracy)—were added as necessary elements, and the various combinations of these activities were discussed as definitions. The final product (definition) of this model becomes as follows (cf. Figure 3-2):

"Certain categories of social work activities related to other countries performed by professional social workers, based on certain values (e.g., human rights, social justice, democracy, the promotion of the profession)."

Period III (Phase IV in the first column) is the time when the future of international social work is questioned under globalization. The entire social work, including 'national' social work, is internationalized/globalized (cf. 2.6 pp. 122-128) and put in an international/global context. Problems, standards and practices of social work are internationalized/globalized. The element of "international"/"global" penetrates every corner of social work and 'national' social work. All people are required to have "international"/"global" eyes (lenses) and be involved in social work.

Thus, international social work ceases to exist, being absorbed into 'national' social work. At the same time, international social work endlessly increases its importance and expands and globalizes the existing mainstream Western-rooted social work to the whole world, with or without indigenization. Social work has become a global profession.

(2) 'A theory of the state' model, Chapter 2-origin

This model (Figure 3-3) is backed up by 'a theory of the state' while owing a debt to the above mainstream model. 'A theory of the state' here is a nickname given to the model which gives its attention to a nation and has its birth and development from a nation state, a sovereign nation, to the welfare state, its limitation, and further to the welfare world, and their relationship with social work. Myrdal's and Pinker's theories were referred in Chapter 2.[48] 'A theory of the state' here does not mean the reference to such grand theories as those of Platōn, Bodin, Spinoza, Rousseau, and Marx.

In the beginning, there is Phase I. International social work is born with the birth of the nation state with national borders. Some areas of social work which had been carried out without being conscious of national borders, naturally could not avoid being outside these borders as they were when national borders were first drawn. At the time, there was not yet any such term as 'international social work,' but there were almost identical international social work activities following the nomenclature in the later phases.

Phase II is the stage when the name 'international social work' is given to those activities. It is the same as "Period 1" of the mainstream model above. The only difference is that activities here do not necessarily need to be ones carried out by social workers.

In Phase III, the "international" social work in Phase II leaps to become "international social work." Nevertheless, "international social work" is not deemed to be certain categories of activities and their combination of categories as in the mainstream model, but is rather deemed to be a certain 'way of viewing matters' (cf. 'value' in the 'mainstream' model). Those categories of activities that do not have such 'a way of viewing matters' are not international social work although they are certainly representative 'candidates' for being considered so.

The content of 'the way of viewing matters' is "eyes (views) from the outside of or beyond nation states," or "eyes (views) from the world," or "compound eyes (multiple views)." Behind this 'way of viewing' there is a

---

48   The later development of their (Myrdal's and Pinker's) theories and other alternative theories for the welfare of all people in the world after 'welfare state' is not referred to in this book.

'secret story' on the second birth of international social work, that is, social work's relation to states (cf. the right column of Figure 3-1, p.91; Figure 3-5, p.112; Figure 3-8, p.124).

Social work, in its development, gradually transfers its activities and functions to a state, which eventually embraces social work. The Welfare State is its ultimate form. Facing the limits of the nation state, international social work breaks through these walls to become an independent entity leaving 'national' social work behind. International social work is now out of the sovereignty of nation states. The tentative final definition of international social work under this model is as follows (cf. Figure 3-3):

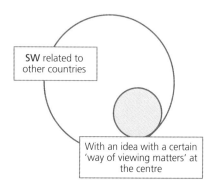

Figure 3-3.
State theory model definition

SW related to other countries

With an idea with a certain 'way of viewing matters' at the centre

SW: Social work

"Social work that is related to other countries, performed by anyone, with a certain 'way of viewing matters', to promote the wellbeing of all people on the earth equally. (No specific importance is put on any specific countries or regions including one's own.)"

Phase IV is the stage when international social work reexamines its own concept and faces self-contradiction in the progress of internationalization and globalization.

International social work will continue to exist as long as nation states and national borders continue. They will not disappear in the near, or even medium future. Internationalization/globalization does not mean the end of nation states.

International social work could be the promoter of the globalization of existing mainstream social work itself, to disseminate itself to the world but also be 'the person standing watch' over its globalization. While mainstream international social work starts with its own social work and makes efforts to disseminate it to the whole world, the international social work of this model starts with social work in an unfixed form and tries to make for a consolidating social work connoting all types of indigenous social work—Buddhist social work, Islamic social work, non-professional NGO social work, social work by country, and the social work of "being indigenous" as defined by the United Nations, as well as mainstream social work.[49] International social work must be linguistically and logically applicable to all people in all countries and regions on the Earth and all kinds of social work. International social work contributes not only to the development of 'national' social work, but also that of the whole of social work to its next stage.

1.2 Brief Discussion on the Achievements of the International Social Work of Western-rooted (Professional) Social Work— Questions Raised at the End of Chapter 1

Six questions from (a) to (f) were raised at the end of Chapter 1 (2 (3) pp.49-50) on 'the final products' (definitions) of mainstream international social

---

49   "[T]he definition of the United Nations and mainstream Western Social Work" is "'native people,' who 'live within geographically distinct ancestral territories (IFSW; Commentary note of IASSW/IFSW Global Definition),' such as Maori, Inuit, and Ainu in (in case of Japan). We treat Buddhist people in Asia as indigenous people...Indigenous people in our usage here are not necessarily associated with Western colonization and hegemony and not necessarily confined as the minority in their current countries (cf. above commentary note) but must have originated in the community, society, area, region or nation in old days although 'how old' they must go back has not rigidly been defined. Included in indigenous social work are Buddhist social work, Islamic social work, Hindu social work, some non-religious social works, Bhutanese social work, Vietnamese social work, Thai social work, etc. as well as social work by indigenous people in the meaning of UN and IFSW's definition above" (Akimoto, et al., 2020: 66-67).

work and on 'international social work under globalization.' Elucidatory discussion on the two models in the subsection immediately above (1.1, pp.89-) has provided us with brief tentative answers to some of the questions and elaborated on some other questions for further discussion in the following Section 2 of this chapter (pp.102-). This is another preparation for the construction of a new international social work. Answers should be integrated into any newly constructed definition of international social work.

(1) Three questions on 'the final products' (definitions) of mainstream international social work

(a) "Is it appropriate for those activities/'functions' which were raised in functional definitions to be called those of international social work?"
The answer to this question was given in the 1995 article published outside the Western, non-English-speaking world (Chapter 2). It listed all activities done under the name of international social work and concluded that they were "not necessarily" international social work. Without certain 'norms' or 'the way of viewing matters,' they are not international social work. The mainstream Western-rooted social work world had replaced 'norms' or 'the way of viewing matters' with 'value' as written in Chapter 1.

(b) "Is it appropriate to include the 'value' elements such as human rights which were mentioned in "value-focused definitions" and "combined definitions" under international social work?"
It may be acceptable to include the 'value' in the definitional factors at its abstract conceptual level if so desired, but the content of the 'value' to be filled in, for example, human rights and social justice, is not appropriate and acceptable in a double meaning. First, they are 'values' of social work as a whole and not specific to international social work, and second, they are the most typical core 'values' of Western-rooted professional social work. One

may or may not accept the common-sense equation Social Work = Western-rooted Professional Social Work. The matter pertains to the understanding/ definition of social work itself, not to international social work which we are now discussing. We are not able to discuss this point here. We shall put it aside for another time (2.1. (1), p.102).

(c) "Must those activities/functions of international social work in "functional definitions" and "combined definitions" be carried out by professional social workers?"

This question also pertains to what social work is, and not what international social work is. See the last few lines in subsection (b) immediately above. International social work does not necessarily have to be carried out by professional social workers unless you believe in the equation above. Social work may be understood more broadly, considering social works in the world—if you distinguish between social work and social workers and also between those people who do social work and social workers who work as a profession, an occupation, or a job. Suppose international social work could be performed only by professional social workers from a Western-rooted social work world, then the great majority of the people on the Earth would be excluded from international social work service, and serve only as an object for international social workers to work on or only if opportunities should be given.

The above functional definition and combined definition have "by professional social workers" as a necessary condition, and the value-focused definition has "any social work in the world" as a necessary condition, but those conditions could be mutually interchangeable between the two types of definitions.

(2) Three questions on "international social work under globalization"

Some of the essence of the answers has already been presented in the last part relating to Phase IV of the section 1.1.(1) and (2) above (pp.92-97). However, some elaboration of the questions will be made, even though there may be some redundancy.

(d) "If the 'local' practice is put in the global context, is the globalized ('local') practice still 'local' social work, or is it international social work? Will international social work continue to exist? If so, what are the roles and functions of international social work which is coexistent with such globalized 'local' social work? What will it look like?"

Everything in society is globalized. Social work is also globalized, and 'local' ('national') social work is globalized, too. Social work and 'local' ('national') social work are put in a globalized context, and global elements penetrate every corner of social work and 'local' ('national') social work. Is, then, the 'local' ('national') practice in a global context or the globalized 'local' ('national') practice still 'local' social work, or is it international social work? Will 'local' ('national') social work absorb and swallow up international social work, and will international social work disappear? If not, what will its roles and functions be, and what will it look like in the future? What will the relationship between international social work with globalized 'local' ('national') social work and the globalized social work be? What we are discussing is "What must international social work under the globalization be?" not "What is 'local' social work under globalization?"

(e) "How does international social work deal with the globalization of social work itself?"
Should 'the final products' (the definitions) that contain the problems questioned in the above subsections (a) to (c) be disseminated to the world as

to do so is one of the conventional roles, functions, and responsibilities of international social work? Social work to be globalized is that of Western-rooted professional social work. It is the globalization of social work itself in the sense of the transfer of matters and standards from the centre to the peripherals. Western-rooted professional social work tends to be critical of globalization because of its negative effects. However, Western-rooted professional social work is indifferent to or even unconscious of the globalization of social work itself in this sense—its values, knowledge, skills, education, and profession—all over the world including the non-Western world. How will international social work deal with this globalization of social work itself? Should international social work reject other forms of social work other than Western-rooted professional social work and disseminate Western-rooted professional social work to the world while it insists on being "international" and of and for the whole world, carrying with it the name of international social work? It would imply a self-contradiction, wouldn't it? How should international social work understand the globalization of Western-rooted professional social work itself?

(f) "What is the contribution of international social work to the development of social work itself to its third stage?"

On the other hand, what contribution will international social work make to the development of 'local' ('national') social work, and social work as a whole? Can social work and 'local' ('national') social work develop to the next stage without international social work and its contribution? Due to the limitation of 'local' ('national') social work, international social work was born from within 'local' ('national') social work. Once it was born, international social work brings in its 'way of viewing matters' and other features and elements to the 'local' ('national') social work and regulates it one way or another. 'Local' ('national') social work, in turn, may shout back to international social work blaming it for its "globalization" but as far as it accepts any, it changes itself and develops, and through the process, social work itself changes and develops. Without the contribution of international social work, not only 'local' ('national') social work but also social work itself, which originated in Europe (Stage I) and matured in North America (Stage II), could not develop into the next stage (Stage III), the stage in which it serves people all over the world.

2. A New Construction of 'International Social Work'

Now it is the time to construct the concept of 'international social work.' We will owe the above two models, the 'mainstream' model and the 'theory of the state' model, particularly heavily the latter, but our construction is not one of the 'theory of the state' model itself. We will mainly try deductively to construct an 'international social work' that would satisfy the lessons we have learned from the above Chapters 1 and 2 and Chapter 3.1, although in social work, the importance of an inductive approach is often emphasized.

2.1 Groundwork

(1) International + social work: putting 'social work' in a black box

When people say that there are a variety of understandings of what international social work is, for the most part, this variety comes from variations in the understanding of the latter half of the term 'international social work,' that is, 'social work.' Almost all people in the social work community in the world today are believers in Western-rooted professional social work. They take the equation 'social work = professional social work' for granted. Both the definition of Healy and that of Cox & Pawar, for example, understand 'international social work' as functions by professional social workers or the aim to promote the profession of social work (Ch.1, pp. 29-34).

There could, however, be other understandings of international social work in the world. Even if we accept the above equation, professional social work in a postindustrial society and that in a pre-industrial society or in a society that is beginning to industrialize could not be the same. Or must social work be defined as the product of industrialization? Social work could vary in content even among "developed" countries and even among "developing" countries, depending on the tradition, culture, and political, economic, and social systems of each country. Even the IASSW/IFSW's global definition, a typical expression of Western-rooted professional social work, pays attention to the diversity among regions. For example, refer to a series of works by Akimoto and his team on Buddhist social work since the early 2010s for further discussion on this topic (e.g., Sakamoto, 2013-15; Sasaki, 2013; Akimoto, 2015, 2017; Akimoto, et al., 2020; Gohori, 2017-2022).

Here, we cannot start by asking the question "What is 'social work'?" The answers would be too varied. Refraining from asking this question, let's continue our discussion assuming that there is more than one kind of social work in the world, particularly as we are now going to discuss 'international social work' that refers to the whole world. We will only leave the understanding and interpretation of this part ('social work') to respective readers—although most of them would understand it to be Western-rooted professional social work—for the time being until we reach the last part of this chapter to make the story simpler. What we should question here is the first part of the term, 'international social work,' that is, the understanding of 'international.'

(2) Inter + national: "nation" as the core and "between"

The word "international" is comprised of two parts, "inter" and "national" ("nation").

(i) Nation

In this chapter, 'nation' is used in the sense of "a country, considered especially about its people and its social or economic structure," and not of "a large group of people of the same race and language." It is used above in the sense of a nation state defined as "a nation that is a politically independent country," (*Longman Dictionary of Contemporary English*, 6th Edition), and not limited to "a sovereign state of which most of the citizens or subjects are united also by factors which define a nation, such as a language or common descent[50]" (*Oxford Dictionary of English*, Second Edition Revised).

The original meaning of the word 'nation' and the history of the birth of modern nation states in Europe would support the second usage in the meaning of races or ethnic groups, and even today, many people in Western societies, especially in its birthplace Europe, may first imagine 'nations' in this sense when they hear the words 'nation,' 'national,' and 'international.' One of the representative definitions of international social work given in Chapter 1 has retained the understanding—that international social work is "social work activities and interest which exceed the borders of state and culture" (Sanders and Pederson, 1984: xiv; underlined by the current author[51]) (underlined by the current author). The meaning of the above has, however, shifted toward the usage of politically independent states, through the history of sovereign nation states in Africa and other regions. (See Box 3-1.)

(ii) Inter-, international, and international social work

The first part of 'international' is 'inter.' The prefix 'inter' means between or among. 'International' literally means "existing, occurring, or carried on between nations" (*Oxford Dictionary of English*, Second Edition Revised) or at the interface between nations.

---

50 Each type of sovereign nation state has its own features to be discussed separately but it is a matter within international social work.

51 Huegler, Lyon & Pawar (2012) uses the term of new "nation states" (p.11).

Box 3-1. Dictionary definitions of international, nation, and nation state

A. International (between a) countries and b) nations)

◆ a) connected with or involving two or more countries (*Oxford Advanced Learner's Dictionary, 8th edition*)

◆ b) existing, occurring, or carried on between nations (*Oxford Dictionary of English, Second Edition Revised*)

◆ b) relating to or involving more than one nation (*Longman Dictionary of Contemporary English, 6th Edition*)

B. Nation a) folk or ethnic group (putting countries aside), b) country or state (being conscious of folk), c). country or state or peoples (without being conscious of folk)

◆ a) a large body of people united by common descent, history, culture, or language, inhabiting a particular state or territory (*Oxford Dictionary of English, Second Edition Revised*)

◆ b) a country, considered especially in relation to its people and its social or economic structure; a large group of people in the same race and language (*Longman Dictionary of Contemporary English, 6th Edition*)

◆ b) a country considered as a group of people with the same language, culture, and history, who live in a particular area under one government; c) all the people in a country (*Oxford Advanced Learner's Dictionary, 8th edition*)

C. *Nation(-)state* transition from a) a state based on folks to b) & c) a state based on sovereignty

◆ a) a group of people with the same culture, language, etc. who have formed an independent country (*Oxford Advanced Learner's Dictionary, 8th edition*)

◆ b) a sovereign state in which most of the citizens or subjects are united also by factors that define a nation, such as language or common descent (*Oxford Dictionary of English, Second Edition Revised*)

- ◆ c) a nation that is a politically independent country (*Longman Dictionary of Contemporary English, 6th Edition*)
- ◆ Modern nations that are formed on the basis of (racial/ethnic) communities...These modern nation states were first formed under monarchy sovereignty, but bourgeois revolution rejected them and instead established the principle of popular sovereignty. In Europe, in the 17th to 19th centuries, these nationalistic movements arose and nation states were formed one after another. This nationalism spread to Asian and African regions around WWI, and the independent movement of anticolonialism arose in various places in the period after World War II. But these countries were at an immature stage of becoming a modern nation in the European sense...Political units which first appeared in the form of racial/ethnic states were not ones whose subjects were single race/ethnic in the strict meaning, and many of them featured mixed racial/ethnic composition. The sovereign nations which have been their basic constituents since the formation of modern international society showed the features of popular states rather than racial/ethical states. . . (*Buritanika kokusai daihyakka jiten* [Britannica International Encyclopedia], *Britannica Japan, 2014*) [English translation by TA.]
- ◆ ...there are no nations which fit the definition as it stands. Firstly, nations which do not embrace the problem of racial/ethnic minorities seldom exist...and, although the formation of nation states are phenomena of modern and present times, there could still be some which could be classified into types which differ in their closeness to the definition...In some countries in the third world which obtained the right to self-determination after World War II, by the liberation from colonial rule, the regional borders have been decided arbitrarily regarding language and culture, and national integration is very weak(*Shin shakaigaku jiten* [New Encyclopedia of Sociology], Yūhikaku, *1993*). [English translation by TA.]

'International social work' is the social work relating to more than a nation in the broadest sense. (Ch1 1.2(2) p.24; 1.3(2) p.31) More than a nation could mean from two neighbouring countries to a few or several countries, to all countries in a region (e.g., South Asia, the Balkan States, Latin America, ASEAN, North Africa, Western Europe) and ultimately up to all 200 countries throughout the world.[52]

(iii) National borders

"National" ("Nation") is the core word, and without "nation," neither "international" nor international social work could linguistically and conceptually be possible. The 'nation' will be sometimes replaced with "national borders" below in this chapter to imply "between nations" and the conceptual and physical limits, to avoid being drawn into a discussion on 'the theory of the state' itself too deeply, and to make the operationalized discussion easier. Sanders and Pederson (1984) cited in the above subsection (i) straightforwardly defined international social work as "social work activities and concerns that transcend national…boundaries."

2.2 Framework

(1) Two types of international social work

International social work is social work related to more than a 'nation' (hereinafter to be sometimes referred to as nation, state, and country interchangeably, although the meaning of these terms is, academically speaking, of course, different and some objections may be raised). In the

---

52   Healy says that international social work in this sense covers a broader range than the expression, 'global social work.' (The 3rd International Academic Forum of the Asian Research Institute for International Social Work (ARIISW), Shukutoku University, held in Tokyo on January 20, 2018.

past, it was enough for social work to take a look within a 'nation.' However, it became necessary to exceed the sovereign nation or national borders due to the internationalization of society. Internationalization presented limits on nation states and thus 'national' social work. ('National' social work here means social work at each nation's level or 'of' or 'in' each nation, not social work administered by a government. In this book, we will use the term 'national' social work although such other expressions might be possible as state social work, local social work, domestic social work, social work country by country, and one's own country's social work.)

There could be two different ways of exceeding national borders, which have given birth to two types of 'international social work.' The difference comes from the disputant's position or from where they start thinking and arguing: one way could be from inside a specific 'nation,' most typically one's own 'nation,' using it as a base for further expansion to provide better service to their cases and policies, and the other from outside individual sovereign nations, keeping equal distance from them and as an independent entity.

In the former, ('national') social work simply extends its activities beyond national borders to provide services, or better services, to people 'in' or 'of' its own nation and to promote the wellbeing of those people. These social work activities that relate to other countries are named here as "international social work (A)." For example, to work for international migrants in the social workers' own country, they will have to work with other countries; and to gain new knowledge and skills, they will have to attend international conferences and exchange research results (Chapter 1).

In the latter, facing the limit of a state, a new entity named here as 'international social work (B)' which separates itself from 'nations' and 'national' social work, is born to provide better services to people not of their own one specific 'nation' but of more than one 'nation,' up to all the 200 'nations' and regions of the world to promote their wellbeing. For example, they will work for the resolution of conflicts between two or more countries,

Figure 3-4. Two ways national borders could be exceeded

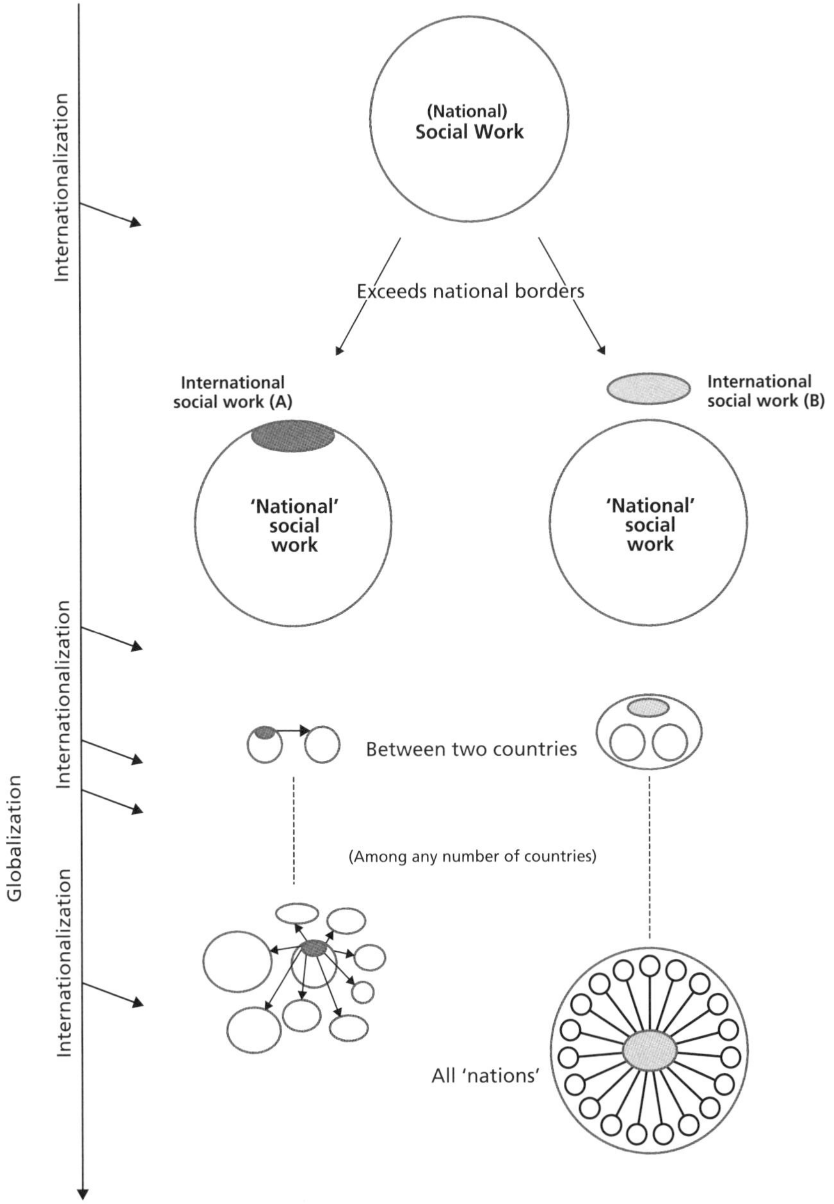

Internationalization
(National)
Social Work
Exceeds national borders
International social work (A)
International social work (B)
'National' social work
'National' social work
Internationalization
Between two countries
Globalization
(Among any number of countries)
Internationalization
All 'nations'

disease prevention, and better working conditions, and may work for the ILO, the Red Cross, or Save the Children, and will put their own country to one side for the time being (cf. the right bottom circle in Figure 3-4).

Both types are beyond the nation state and its limits but while the former aims to promote the well-being of the people of a nation state, the latter aims to promote the wellbeing of peoples of more than a state or all states in the world, which are outside of its own state. The former concerns itself with other states and 'national' social work following its own needs while the latter first sets itself up as a separate entity from each nation state and 'national' social work, and concerns itself with each nation state and 'national' social work. The latter sees things by viewing and considering them all as a whole.

The former, 'international social work (A),' is of, by, and for its own 'nation' and its people, and thus is fundamentally part of a 'national' social work however closely it works with other countries. We hereinafter call the latter, i.e., 'international social work (B),' as International Social Work (with capitalized initials).

(2) Nations and International Social Work: structural elements of social work and their locational relationship

Figure 3-5 shows the structural elements of social work (International Social Work, 'national' social work, and social work as a whole) and the locational relationship among them. Social work is composed of 'national' social work (small white circles with dark gray ovals within) and International Social Work (a gray oval), which is an independent entity segregated from 'national' social work. In other words, the two parts, 'national' social work and International Social Work, have come together to make up social work. The lower right figure is this observation from the point of view of 'national' social work.

Figure 3-5. Locational relationships among international social work, 'national' social work and social work

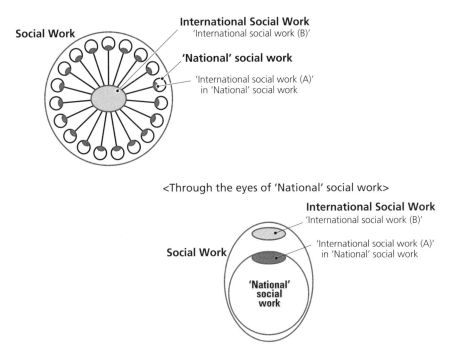

<Through the eyes of 'National' social work>

2.3 Core elements of International Social Work

We proceed with the inquiry and the construction of International Social Work in the meaning of 'international social work (B).'

Core elements of International Social Work are (a) to (d) below. International Social Work is not special. It is part of social work as a whole just as 'national' social work is. Purposes, principles, values, and other elements of International Social Work are basically the same as those of 'national' social work. Suppose 'social work' = 'Western-rooted professional social work'—although we put social work in a black box at the beginning of this section (2.1(1) p.102)—the purpose would be to alleviate and solve the difficulties and problems in people's lives and promote their wellbeing (see IASSW/IFSW Global Definition). The fundamental principles or values of both International Social Work and 'national' social work are social justice and human rights. The field of actual practice of International Social Work would be both inside and outside of the practitioner's own country. It is also the same as in 'national' social work, which is practiced by social workers both inside and outside of their home country.

Consistency with the core elements involved in 'national' social work is first required. But stepping into a new field of "international" or introducing the new ingredient of national borders, some revisions and additions may become necessary. This is nothing unique to the topic of "international." It is also the case with other new fields[53] and when new ingredients are introduced. The major revisions and additions to International Social Work are as follows ((a) to (d)). Possible items that may be still hidden or items with a potential of which we have been unaware will become evident sometime in the future.

(a) The key term

The key term in 'International Social Work' is 'between nations' or 'national borders.'[54] The modern sovereign nation forms the core of our inquiry on 'international social work.' The antonym[55] of International Social Work is 'national' social work with national borders.

---

53 In Chapter 1, it was written that international social work was not a field, but the meaning is different here.

54 Sanders and Pederson (1984), "social work activities and concerns that transcend national and cultural boundaries (1.2 (2) p. 100)."

55 To extract the essence of "international social work," we should provide an antonym.

(b) The task

The task of International Social Work is social work beyond or related to national borders in problems, standards or practices[56] (See p.17; Ch.1 and Ch.3.1).

(c) Constituency

Constituents, or the target population, of International Social Work, are all people (eight billion; UN *World Population Prospects 2022*) in all countries and regions (about 200 as of 2022) of the world, not simply the people in one's own nation.

(b) + (c) Purpose

The purpose of International Social Work is to alleviate and solve the difficulties and problems in people's lives and to promote the well-being of people all over the world, not only those of the people in one's own country.

(d) 'The way of viewing matters'

International Social Work's greatest feature is its certain 'way of viewing matters.' 'The way of viewing matters' in the literal sense could connote value, which the mainstream Western-rooted professional social work referred to in Chapter 1 as such, the purpose and the aim, the principle, the philosophy, the ideology, and perception. 'The way of viewing matters' could be interpreted as a 'yardstick' (ruler, measure, or standard) in an operationalized form.

But the content of 'the way of viewing matters' specifically here is 'the way of looking at things' with eyes from the outside or more than one pair of eyes. International Social Work views matters by leaving behind and not sticking to a specific nation, most typically one's own country. It does not see

---

56   Also concepts and theories (Akimoto, 1992).

things through putting one's own country or people at the centre.

International Social Work does not look at things with a single yardstick but does so by applying two yardsticks or more, which could hopefully be developed into a common yardstick for the use of all parties. Looking at the thinking in Western-rooted professional social work, conventions of the United Nations and its affiliated and related organizations as well as human rights, social justice, and other concepts could be examples of those common yardsticks, (cf. Friedlander, 1975) although they are not necessarily the common yardsticks we mean here. Ours exceeds these levels, eliminating value factors as much as possible. The following two considerations should be made.

(i) Social work without 'the way of viewing matters'

Firstly, unless it passes this test of having 'the way of viewing matters' or yardsticks, we cannot refer to or define any social work activities as International Social Work even if these activities are related to other countries. They are 'national' social work, which aims at the promotion of the well-being of one's own nation and people.

The items that were listed in Chapter 2 (pp.67-71) as "these are not necessarily international social work" are not necessarily "these are not International Social Work" (in capitals). If they pass the test of 'the way of viewing matters', they are International Social Work. The point is that we do not call anything International Social Work unless it has been screened by 'the way of viewing matters' above.

(ii) Erasing national borders

In other words, the core meaning of 'the way of viewing matters' of "International Social Work" is to regard all nations and peoples or all people and their groups at an equal distance regardless of their nationalities. International Social Work does not give specific values to any specific nations or peoples. We regard them as being the same even while they are different.[57] It does not attach a label of either superiority or inferiority to any specific states or peoples. Just think of the clamor for the superiority of the so-called Germanic race, the Anglo-Saxon race, the Han race, the Yamato race, etc., even when replacing 'race' with 'nation' and 'people.'

Ultimately, if one views matters by erasing national borders, a very different world may come to the fore. We would see the world using class, race, gender, religion, language, functional communities as well as other indices before national borders or nationality.[58] People may insist on using such terms as "world citizens,"[59] "Earthians," and "being human beings," although they are not theoretically, historically, or legally plausible at present or in the near future.

In reality, national borders firmly exist—however far internationalization and globalization proceed, and people, things, money, information, etc., break down national borders here and there (Akimoto, 2004). Even main players in "international social work," e.g., the United Nations, nation states, international NGOs, religious organizations, multi-corporations, independent firms, and individuals and their groups, are not free from national interest and nationality.

---

57   If they are the same and single, the cooperation, collaboration, and joint work could not become a topic to discuss. Both journeys to seek not for differences but for sameness and not for sameness but for differences would start.

58   During periods of war today, these factors are subdued under nationality.

59   The concept of citizenship requires a government that responds to their rights. A world government has not yet come into being.

(a) + (b) + (c) + (d) The idea (*idee*)[60]

'The idea (*idee*)' will be used below in this chapter as the roundup concept of (a) to (d) above. It could include a historical perspective for the future and dreams.[61] The meaning of the idea (*idee*) here is close to one in philosophy[62] rather than one in daily life—a "thought or suggestion as to a possible course of action" (*Oxford Dictionary of English*, 2nd Ed. Revised, Oxford University Press, 2005).

2.4 Birth of International Social Work and the Historical Development of its Relation with 'National' Social Work and Social Work as a Whole

Here we throw in the time factor.

(i) The first birth

Without nation states, no international social work would have been plausible, not only linguistically but also historically. The birth of international social work owes much to the birth and the existence of modern sovereign nation states, which are defined by 'people,' 'sovereignty,' and 'territory.' National borders embody the conceptual and physical limits of nation states. Logically speaking, 'international social work' was born when national borders were born. Some of the social work activities until that moment might remain (a) outside the newly-drawn national borders as they

---

60   *Rinen*. "The idea which transcends experiences. The fundamental thought of how the matter is to be" *Japanese Language Dictionary*, Shōgakukan, 2006). "It is used as the purpose for decision and interpretation without the ontological implication" (*Kōjien*, ver.6, Iwanami Shoten, 2008, 2014).

61   Cf. Footnote 49 on p.97.

62   "Philosophy" (in Platonic thought) is an externally existing pattern of which individual things in any class are imperfect copies: (in Kantian thought) a concept of pure reason, not empirically based in experience" (*Oxford Dictionary of English*, 2nd Ed. Revised, Oxford University Press, 2005).

had been, or (b) as some contacts and activities beyond national borders from the need to provide services to their domestic clients inside the newly-drawn national borders (cf. 'international social work (A)'). This was the first birth of international social work. Social work before this moment had nothing to do with or no consciousness of national borders.

(ii) The second birth—spin-off and boomerang

International Social Work, 'international social work (B),' was born from another limit of ('national') social work[63] as a spin-off (1) in Figure 3-6). This is the second birth of 'international social work.' Once it was born, the newly-born international social work boomeranged to intrude into 'national' social work. It started and continued conveying its core elements (cf. the above section 2.3 pp.112-117) including 'the way of viewing matters' as well as various other thoughts and practices with 'the way of viewing matters' implied to 'national' social work (2) in Figure 3-6). 'National' social work may accept, resist, or reject them together with the messages and demands International Social Work sends in (3) in Figure 3-6). As far as it accepts any of them, however, those accepted become part of its 'national' social work and the social work itself, and contribute to the change and the development of 'national' social work, and eventually the change and the development of social work itself to the next stage (4) in Figure 3-6). In the case of Western-rooted professional social work, the next stage means its third stage in which it will serve the whole world after the first stage (birth in Europe) and the second stage (growth in North America).

---

63 Strictly speaking, "'national' social work" could be said to have been born as a result of the birth of "International Social Work." Until then, it was "social work."

Figure 3-6. The birth and boomerang effect of International Social Work

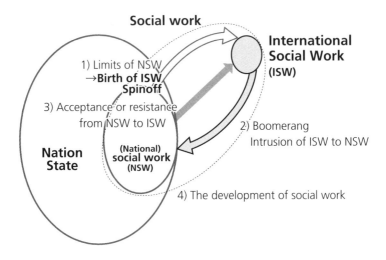

(iii) The existence outside of sovereignty

However, the biggest treasure which this circular movement has left us was the birth of International Social Work which is located outside the sovereignty of any nation and 'national' social work, but within social work. Now as social work is composed of 'national' social work and International Social Work, it essentially includes the part that is outside the sovereignty of any nation states.

2.5 The *Idealtypus*[64] and the 'Actual Being': International Social Work and International Social Work´(dash)

Hereinbefore, the discussion was mainly held at the *Idealtypus* (ideal type; philosophy) level. We had dropped the factor of 'actual being' as much as possible up to this point.

Now, we throw in this factor. International Social Work in an actual society cannot be free from individual nation states and 'national' social work in actual societies. International Social Work in actual society has been distorted from the ideal type of International Social Work under construction above. We call this distorted International Social Work as International Social Work´(dash) (hereinafter to be referred to as International Social Work´(dash)) in this chapter.

Firstly, International Social Work is structurally composed of 'national' social works of all states, which are different in size and power. All nation states are looking out for their own national interest, and each 'national' social work works for the benefit of its own people whom it serves. Secondly, not only structurally but also in the process of daily operation, International Social Work in an actual society is always under those nations and 'national' social work with the differences in power and does not function neutrally. International Social Work´(dash) has skewed towards 'national' social work of nations with power in their administration and operation. (Figure 3-7)

---

64 A methodological concept in social sciences by Max Weber. "Types or models made of essential factors which were selected from among many phenomena to measure, compare or evaluate real cultural phenomena which are very fluid and scattered" (Japanese Dictionary (Nihon Kokugo Daijiten), Shōgakukan, 2006) (English translation by TA).

Figure 3-7. International Social Work´(dash): International Social Work in the actual society

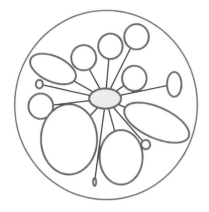

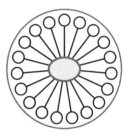

Cf. International
Social Work

The actual existing International Social Work is not that of the pure ideal international social work presented in the above subsection 2.3, but a distortion of that, even if it may pretend to be equal in distance from all nations. However, International Social Work exists holding the above-mentioned idea (above 2.3, p.116) as an impregnable tower and directs the actual existing distorted International Social Work´(dash) towards an ideal International Social Work.

'National' social work on the opposite pole makes an effort to bring International Social Work closer to itself for its own interest, but it cannot help but consider, and has considered, the idea of International Social Work. International Social Work´(dash) is in a tug of war between International Social Work and 'national' social work, which have different starting points and goals.

Metaphorically, think of the United Nations. The United Nations exists outside individual sovereign states as an independent organization. Nevertheless, the United Nations is structurally composed of individual sovereign states which have different sizes and powers and operates under its organizational conditions. While those individual sovereign states have sought and fought for their national interests and benefits, they have also worked together and cooperated and collaborated through compromise. The Universal Declaration of Human Rights and many conventions are, for example, regarded as the highest-level common yardsticks that were agreed to by all or the majority of sovereign states, but, in reality, they were adopted and have been administered by those member states with a greater voice and power and in specific historical, political and social conditions. Nevertheless, the existence of the United Nations is generally regarded as being fair, valuable, and indispensable by the majority of states.

2.6 Environmental Factors: Internationalization and Globalization

Both factors of time and actual existence are thrown in.

(1) The internationalization of society and social work

Behind the story from the second birth of International Social Work to the boomerang in the section 2.4 (pp.116-118), the current of internationalization flowed, although to be more exact, it had been running ever since the first birth of 'international social work,' that is, the formation of nation states and national borders.

Internationalization "[o]riginally" means "to show the relative relation between countries," but the definition varies. A few examples of common usage of the word are: (a) "To transform a nation from a self-sufficient, closed system to an interdependent, coexistent system"; (b) "To assume its own due

share of obligation and responsibility to stand abreast with other nations";
and (c) "Widely to open the door to the world for the inflow of people, things,
culture, information, etc. from other nations" (*Britannica International
Encyclopedia (Buritanika Kokusai, Dai-hyakkajiten*), Britannica Japan, 2014).
[English translation by TA.]

Society has been internationalized, politically, economically, and socially.
Social work, which is part of it, is no exception. The internationalization of
society internationalized social work in two ways. Firstly, it facilitated the
birth and growth of International Social Work. Secondly, it put 'national'
social work in an internationalized context and infused it with an
"international" element in all its aspects.

(2) The internationalization of 'national' social work

(i) The three drives of the internationalization of 'national' social work
The internationalization of 'national' social work has come about in three
ways: 1. extending itself outwards to satisfy with immediate needs of its own
clients and with interests of its own and its own state for more knowledge
and better services; 2. becoming a "good international" state to be accepted
with respect by other states; and 3. being required and forced to change by
outside forces.

---

65 We believe that no nation is responsible to itself alone, but that laws of political morality
    are universal; and that obedience to such laws is incumbent upon all nations who would
    sustain their own sovereignty and justify their sovereign relationship with other nations.

Figure 3-8. Internationalization by society in general and International Social Work

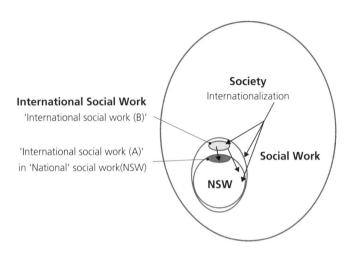

Regarding 1., we may remember the description of the birth of 'international social work (A)' (2.2 (1) p.108 and 2.4 pp.116- above). Regarding 1. and 2., refer to (a) and (b) (pp.122-123) of the definition of internationalization in the immediate above subsection 2.6 (1) and also to the first two terms of the qualification to be "a good person of today" which was mentioned in Chapter 2 (5.(2) p.80)—being a good citizen (national), a good international[ly-minded] citizen, and a good world citizen at a time. The requirement and the force in 3. come both from the society directly and through International Social Work which was born through the internationalization of society. (Figure 3-8)

These 1. to 3. are not necessarily in a time series. International Social Work facilitates and reinforces each of these three steps of the internationalization of 'national' social work above, together with society in general (Figure 3-6).

(ii) The whole 'national' social work is fully internationalized

Problems that social work works for are internationalized, standards (yardsticks) that social work uses are internationalized, and actual practices that social work is engaged in are all internationalized (Ch.1 1.3(3-1), pp.34-35).[66] All subfields of social work, e.g., child welfare, disabilities, the elderly, poverty, and mental health, are internationalized. Even the basic classes on child welfare and disabilities, for example, could not be completed without referring to the UN's Conventions on the Rights of the Child and the Rights of Persons with Disabilities respectively, and the situation of other countries both at the policy and program level and the reality level.[67] 'National' social work must be considered and practiced in the social context of internationalization. Otherwise, nothing in social work could be understood and achieved effectively.

(iii) The substance of internationalization and globalization: one-directional

'National' social work may be willing, reluctant or forced to accept those messages and demands and to be internationalized. The term 'internationalization' was originally a neutral concept used to describe a phenomenon (2.6 (1) pp.121-122 above), but the substance of internationalization tends to be one-directional—from social work "developed countries," that is, the North or the West, to social work "developing countries," that is, the South or non-the West.[68]

The latter copies the former with longing and admiration or obeys the former with humiliation. The sense of imperialism and colonialism may be implied (cf. ACWelS (Asian Center for Welfare Society)'s Internationalization-

---

66   Concepts are, too.

67   For example, the Americans with Disabilities Act (ADA), advanced policies and practices for the elderly people in Sweden, and mass poverty in the world.

68   See the usage of the term 'international social work' in Bhutan, Vietnam, and Thailand in Chapter 1, and in Japan also in Chapter 1.

Indigenization research project (Matsuo 2014) supported the findings).

This "one directional" quality in internationalization has been taken over by the discussion on globalization. Since around the 1990s, the word globalization began being used, overlapping with the word internationalization, and sometimes replacing it interchangeably or overriding unconsciously in the mainstream international social work community even though the meaning and concept of both words are, of course, different.

There are various definitions of globalization, but a definition by Ohno fits our discussion here:

> Globalization does not simply mean the situation whereby each country intensifies contact and competition through trade, investment, finance, information, and personal exchange. Each period of the world's economy has its own geographical and industrial centre. Globalization is a process, with a clear direction and hierarchical structure, in which values and systems of the country at the centre diffuse to other regions by following and coercion. It is "self-evident" in the central country's eyes that their civilization is superior. Globalization implies both the sense of superiority and the sense of mission to extend the benefits to regions that have not yet enjoyed them. Furthermore, it is undeniable that globalization has a side whereby the central country forces other countries to participate in fields where it has an advantage under the rules it has laid down, and reproduces its superiority on a progressive scale. [Translated by the current author.]

> Ohno, K. 2000. *Globalization of Developing Countries—Is the self-sustainable development possible?* Tōyō Keizai Shinpōsha.

That which was written on internationalization in the first paragraph in (iii) on the previous page (p.124) could be simply repeated if the word 'internationalization' were to be replaced with the word 'globalization.' The only notable difference from internationalization is the emphasis on the more explicit and conscious one-directional relationship with the centre (sender) and peripherals (receiver), overriding the euphemism of internationalization. Once, even unipolar theory was in fashion (cf. Akimoto, 2006: 686-690). In the case of social work, what is at the center is the social work of "developed" countries or Western-rooted professional social work.

(3) International Social Work under internationalization and globalization

The discussion in subsections (1) and (2) above was mostly about 'national' social work under internationalization and globalization. Here we shall be discussing the relation of internationalization/globalization to International Social Work, not that of internationalization/globalization to 'national' social work.

International Social Work was facilitated by the environmental condition of the internationalization of a society in its birth and growth, but 'international social work,' in turn, facilitated the internationalization/ globalization of 'national' social work (and even the internationalization/ globalization of the society).

International Social Work brings in 'national' social work not only 1) its 'way of viewing matters' and various thoughts and practices under it but also 2) what is one-directional under internationalization and at the centre under globalization, namely, Western-rooted professional social work. 'Value' tends to be the subject most frequently referred to but knowledge and skills could also be so.

'National' social work retorts in the voice of "Globalization!," "Westernization!," "Social work imperialism!," and "Professional colonialism!," beyond "Domestic interference!" some years ago, in response to what has been brought in, and also against International Social Work (and the society) which had been the agency of this importation. More accurately speaking,

International Social Work is a promoter of internationalization 1) in the paragraph immediately above and a preventer of 2) 'International Social Work' may be a mover for both internationalization 1) and 2) Some people involved in international social work in the Western-rooted professional social work community even promote it as a "global profession" without hesitation under the name of International Social Work.

What we have been exploring is what International Social Work is, and not what specifically the international social work of Western-rooted professional social work is. What we have been interested in with International Social Work is that it can be commonly applicable to or intimate with all social work and all parts of the world. We cannot discuss International Social Work without considering the international social work of other types of social work including Buddhist social work, Islamic social work, various NGO's social work, and as well as other indigenous social work.[69] We sealed the inquiry of what social work is in a black box at the beginning of this section. International Social Work aims to deliver social work to all eight billion people of all countries and regions around the world.

2.7 The Future: Unsolved Questions

(1) Will International Social Work cease to exist?

'National' social work was put in the internationalized context and had the "international" element in every corner of itself (2.6 (1) p.122). 'National' social work is supposed to be fully internationalized. Then, will international social work become unnecessary and cease to exist? This was one of the questions raised at the end of Chapter 1, and discussed briefly in 1.2 (2) (d) in this chapter (p.100). As far as the International Social Work we are

---

69   See footnote 49 p.976.

constructing is concerned, the answer is simply "No" although the name of the 'international social work (A)' (2.2 (1) p.108) may,[70] conceptually, losing its distinction from other parts of 'national' social work.

International Social Work will not cease to exist unless sovereign states cease to exist. Neither International Social Work nor International Social Work´(dash) will disappear shortly while national borderlines have been changing from solid lines to broken lines, and the spaces between the broken lines have been becoming wider. Some may argue that the original question "Will 'international' social work cease to exist?" should have rather been "Will 'national' social work cease to exist?" But the answer and reasoning to this new question would not change.

As long as a nation state continues to exist—it will—and as long as a world state is not born—it will not—International Social Work will be necessary. The role and function of International Social Work will be the same as today: 1. carrying the torch of the original idea of International Social Work, and 2. managing International Social Work (actual International Social Work) as a field of cooperation, collaboration, competition, and compromise, whereas 'national' social work tries to work in its own interests while partly understanding the idea of International Social Work.

Imagine the governing boards of the United Nations and IASSW (International Association of Schools of Social Work). The United Nations is composed of individual sovereign nation states, which compete and compromise national interests in reality and pursue UN ideas. Think of the board members of the IASSW—executive officers and board members elected by the general member body and board members sent in as national representatives. From which side do you see matters, the UN or IASSW side or the individual member country's side? In reality, some executive members may work as if they were national representatives for their own countries,

---

70   Or may not, or maybe even strengthened.

with various degrees. However much their original ideas are distorted, they have their own significance of existence. However much actual International Social Work´(dash) is distorted, it exists as International Social Work.

(2) Are there any common yardsticks that could avoid this criticism of globalization?

Internationalization/globalization forces us to see what is at the centre or the strongest, as common yardsticks crossing national borders or even as global standards. The makeup of globalization in our case is Western-rooted professional social work or its values, knowledge, and skills. 'International Social Work' possibly functions as its promoter while 'national' social work raises the objection of "Globalization!"

Are there any yardsticks common worldwide that could dodge the criticism of globalization? If there are, how can we find them? Indigenization cannot be the answer. What was indigenized is still Western-rooted professional social work. Some minor modifications would have to be made in quality or quantity to make the substantive whole body accepted (seeing from the sender's side), or to accept it (seeing from the receiver's side). (See the ABC Model in Buddhist social work and its extension in Akimoto, 2017: 22-23 and 2020: 65-68.)

Should we think not from the self or the center but from others or the peripheral, that is, indigenous social work in our case? Some common yardsticks may be found if we observe such social work to identify and isolate their yardsticks and consolidate them inductively and all-inclusively.

Or shall we return to the society before national borders were born while we are looking for common yardsticks usable in the society after the national borders were solidly drawn, overcoming, and erasing them?

See Figure 3-9. At one time, in each locality "social work" existed although the term social work was not used. It was 'indigenous' social work. No national borders existed physically and/or within consciousness (I in the Figure). Nation states and national borders were born. Social work was divided into two parts, outside and inside the borders. Most were located inside, within a nation (II in the Figure).

Social work became nationalized although the understanding of social work same as in II could be maintained as far as the way of seeing 'social work before a nation.' Social work gradually transferred some part of its activities to the nation (III in the Figure). "National social work" in the meaning of social work by governments (hereinafter to be referred as "state social work"), not in the meaning of social work geographically bound to a territory, was born and grew. It was gradually institutionalized and eventually embraced, subsumed, and confined by the nation.[71] The welfare state and professionalization and national licensing/certificate programs may be the symbolic culmination. Social work becomes subordinate and even a tool of states (III→IV in the Figure).[72]

During this process, international social work spun off from 'national social work' with the limit of national borders, to be created as an independent entity, which is not under the sovereignty of nation states.

---

71 The speed and the degree of embracement, subsumption, and confinement vary in each nation's social work. Some parts of social work could remain outside 'state social work' while remaining inside 'national social work' as far as the individual identity as social work is preserved.

72 In a more historically accurate picture, the attachment on the right shoulder of IV (cf. Figure 3-6) could be attached to III.

Figure 3-9. Social work and nations and international social work

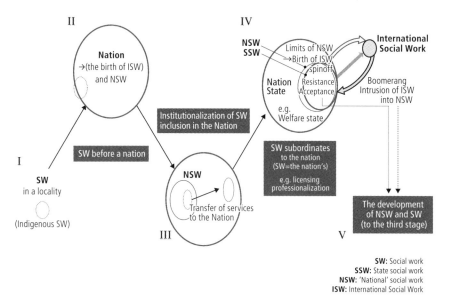

SW: Social work
SSW: State social work
NSW: 'National' social work
ISW: International Social Work

We may find some primitive fundamental common yardsticks applicable to all levels of societies including indigenous societies (I). No killing, no stealing,[73] goodwill, love and compassion, charity, voluntary work without expecting returns,[74] humanism, philanthropy, and social care, for example, might be candidates for those yardsticks although they are certainly too primitive. "They are not social work," would be a spontaneous response from people involved in mainstream Western-rooted professional social work. Social work must be only theirs. "Social work" has not been patented for monopolization by Western-rooted professional social work, which is not serving and cannot serve all people, in all parts of the world.

We are discussing distinguishing social work and those who serve in the field of social work. Among them, there could be social workers who are

---

73   Cf. the Ten Christian Commandments, and the Five Buddhist Commandments.

74   From this point of view, professional social workers, who work for money or as a job, are not those who are doing social work, and professional social work is not social work.

engaged in social work as a job, and among them, there could be professional social workers. (1.2 (1) (c) p.99)

Again, "what social work is" is not the topic of this book. We put this issue in a black box at the very beginning of this section (cf. The 4th International Academic Forum on Buddhist Social Work, December 20-21, Tokyo, Japan; Gohori, J. (Ed.) (2020; 2021)). We are not discussing the International Social Work of Western-rooted professional social work. Our International Social Work must be applicable to all social work. This way of viewing matters, erasing national borders and nationalities, may have been rooted in social work as if it were a DNA molecule. We will see and think of a totally different world to find highly common yardsticks.

3. A Newly Constructed Definition and Conclusive Summary

(1) A Definition of International Social Work

Though still tentative, the construction work has been completed, giving us the following definition of International Social Work[75]:

International Social Work[1] is social work[2] beyond, crossing, or relating to national[3] borders, and being backed up by certain ideas[4]. The constituency comprises all people of all countries and regions worldwide[5], and the aim is to promote their wellbeing. 'The way of viewing matters'[6] is to see with eyes from the outside of nation states including one's own country, with 'compound'[7] eyes, or with more than one or a common yardstick(s).

---

[75] As far as a definition is concerned, minimizing factors and components could make it more inclusive in content while paraphrasing them would be also necessary to guide readers to a better understanding.

International Social Work does not give any special importance, superiority or inferiority, to any specific countries or regions, peoples or nationalities.[8] The antonym of International Social Work is 'national' social work.[9] International Social Work is to be commonly compatible with all indigenous[10] social work.[11]

1) 'International social work (B)' (2.2 (1) p.108)
2) The social work that each reader assumed and put in a black box at the beginning of the previous Section 2.1 (1) p.102). Not necessarily limited to Western-rooted professional social work.
3) Includes "regional" in the equivalent sense to "national"
4) Includes philosophy, principle, value, purpose, aim, yardstick, measure, norm, etc.
5) Not people of one's own country and region. 'Nation' was mainly used in the body of the work, but 'country' is used here for easier understanding.
6) The way of looking at things, purpose and aim, value, yardstick, measure, standard, perspective, approach, etc.
7) 'multifaceted'
8) Other elements within and outside of the idea are not different from those of social work as a whole as International Social Work is part of it, together with 'national' social work.
9) 'National' social work here means social work in each country, not by a government.
10) The usage is different from UNESCO/IFSW definitions (cf. the footnote 49 p. 97).
11) Not only for Western-rooted professional social work. It is to have an affinity for social works as a locomotive is connected to a variety of different cars. Cf. compatibility in grafting.

The keyword of International Social Work is "national borders," and the task is social work crossing or concerning national borders. The constituency comprises eight billion[76] people of some 200 countries and regions, not a specific country or its people, particularly one's own. The purpose is to promote the well-being of the whole world. 'The way of viewing matters,' the core of the idea, is to see with eyes from the outside of sovereign states including one's own country, or with multifaceted eyes, and to use multiple or common yardsticks. Besides this, nothing (values, principles, fields of practice, etc.) is different in International Social Work from 'national' (local;

76 As of the end of 2022.

domestic; state) social work—at this moment although something different might be identified in the future—as both are part of the same social work.

The antonym of International Social Work is 'national' social work, i.e., social work in each country. International Social Work does not give any special importance, superiority, or inferiority to any specific countries or peoples. Representative actors of International Social Work are trans- or inter-governmental organizations, and international nongovernmental organizations including social work organizations but that could also be any groups and any individuals as far as they hold the above-mentioned idea. The idea here has been used as an inclusive term of the constituency, 'the way of viewing matters,' philosophy, its future direction as well as values, principles, purposes, aims, standards, norms, yardsticks, measures, and other elements.

International Social Work has a common affinity with all social works throughout the world and must be compatible with them. 'Social work' here is not limited to Western-rooted social work but could be any other type of social work. Professionalism and human rights, for example, which the Western-rooted social work cherishes as their purpose and value, are applicable as international social work of Western-rooted professional social work, but may or may not be in such other international social works as the international social work of Buddhist social work, Islamic social work, NGO social work, and other indigenous social work. The meaning of "indigenous" here is different from the UNESCO/IFSW definitions. (cf. the footnote 49 p.97)

(2) An opening tour of the new edifice (Summary: Some features of the new International Social Work)

Lastly, let's take our International Social Work visitors on an opening tour to show them some features of the new edifice.

1) All social work related to other countries is not necessarily International Social Work.

All social work related to other countries is not necessarily International Social Work. The meaning is two-fold.

1)-1 Only certain activities with a certain idea

Only certain activities with a certain idea (See the next item 2).) among activities related to other countries are called International Social Work. International social work once leapt from "international" social work to "international social work." In the former, "international" was an adjective to modify 'social work' and meant all 'related to other countries' while in the latter, 'international' is a constituent of an independent three-word term or concept, "international social work." Exploring the concept led to this conclusion above. (cf. In mainstream social work, a category or a combination of categories of social work activities (acts; functions) with a certain value, by professional social workers, were and are called international social work.)

1)-2 There are two kinds of 'international social work,' but one is essentially 'national' social work

There are two ways for social work to exceed national borders: (A) 'National' social work spreads its wings to cross national borders to serve clients of their own countries better and more efficiently. We refer to it as 'international social work (A).' Think of the cases of migrants and international adoption. (B) An independent entity outside 'national' social works is set up to overview all 'national' social works or all people in the world. We refer to this as 'international social work (B).' Think of conventions and activities by the ILO, WHO, International NGOs, and some individuals. We regard 'international social work (A)' as part of 'national' social work in the sense that it focuses on the benefits of people of one's own country. We regard 'international social work (B)' as International Social Work, which sees it with eyes from the outside of nation states including one's own countries.

2) The Idea: For all people of all countries and seeing with eyes from the outside of one's own country

The "idea" in above 1)-1 is a term inclusive of various elements, but in International Social Work, the following two are core elements:

- The constituency: all people in all countries and regions of the world; and
- with eyes from the outside of nation states including one's own country, multifaceted eyes, or multiple or common yardsticks.

In short, it is seeing all peoples and countries as equal, and exceeding national borders, which coincides with the conclusion in above 1)-2.

The background theory[77] is a theory of the state—the understanding of the birth and limits of modern nation states, the distance of the welfare state to the welfare world, and the erasure of national borders. The terms 'world citizen,' 'cosmopolitan,' 'Earthian,' and 'being a human being' toward which International Social Work has its orientation, help us with the construction of this concept although the criticism that they are super-historical and unscientific concepts cannot be avoided.

3) International Social Work of the ideal type and actual existence

International Social Work in an actual society has been distorted from the International Social Work of the ideal type. International Social Work has been structured, administered, and operated on a set of 'national' social works actually existing in the world with different sizes of power. We call this International Social Work International Social Work´ with a dash.

International Social Work´(dash) in actual society is located somewhere

---

77   It is based on the discussion of Western philosophy.

between two poles: International Social Work of the ideal type, and crude 'national' social work working for the benefit of domestic cases in their own countries. A tug of war has been played out between both poles.

While International Social Work´(dash) has grown up along with a trend toward internationalization, it has, in turn, contributed to the internationalization of social work[78] and furthermore to the globalization of social work, that is, the dissemination of Western-rooted professional social work from the center to the peripherals. It is, in a sense, the contribution of International Social Work´(dash) to the distortion of International Social Work itself. The counterattacks from 'national' social work come under the voices of "Globalization!" and "Westernization!" against the force of mainstream Western-rooted professional social work.

Refer to the analogy of the United Nations, which is composed of individual nation states with their different sizes and powers. It contains the idea of peace and prosperity for the whole world but the reality has been distorted by the differences of size and power of each country in structure, administration, and operation.

4) International Social Work is for all social work, not only of Western-rooted
   social work

International Social Work is of all people of all countries of the world and all forms of social work which may exist already and/or latently in the world. It is not only of Western-rooted social work. For example, human rights and professionalization could be acceptable as a value and a purpose, as part of the idea, as far as we discuss international social work at the level of International Social Work of Western International Social Work, but they may or may not be acceptable once we begin discussing International Social Work at the world level, which covers and considers the whole world.

78　It was originally neutral.

International Social Work and its idea must have a universal connection to various other types of social work throughout the world as if it were a locomotive that could be connected to a variety of different railway cars. International Social Work must have an affinity with all social work. The expression of the International Social Work of Western-rooted social work, the International Social Work of Islamic, Buddhist, or NGOs' social work…is linguistically and conceptually self-contradictory.[79]

5) The future

5)-1 Will International Social Work cease to exist?

Will International Social Work vanish if internationalization/globalization proceeds?

If society is internationalized/globalized, 'national' social work will be put in an internationalized/globalized context, the element of "international"/ "global" will penetrate every corner of 'national' social work, and 'national' social work will be internationalized/globalized. The concept of 'National' social work may diminish itself, in the sense of the loss of its uniqueness, by accepting and embodying the idea of International Social Work. But this is a matter of 'national' social work under internationalization/globalization.

What we must discuss here is the destiny of International Social Work under internationalization/globalization. International Social Work ('international social work (B)' p.108) will continue to exist as long as nation states continue to do so[80] although 'international social work (A)' may disappear in the sense that the distinction between it and other parts of 'national' social work will blur and disappear. The role and function of

---

79   (We are not able to go into the subject of 'what social work is' here, besides confessing that we are not believers in the equation, "social work = Western-rooted professional social work" (cf. 1.2 (1) (b) p.98).

80   Even if the solid line denoting national borders on maps is broken into a dotted line and the distance between the dots becomes wider.

International Social Work will continue being to fill the gap between International Social Work and International Social Work´(dash) and orient International Social Work´(dash) towards International Social Work of an ideal type, carrying the torch of the ideal type of International Social Work.

5)-2 Out of sovereign nations and the contribution to the development of social work

The significance of International Social Work is to have located itself outside nation states, or 'national' social work, and to have remained within social work. Social work is now composed of 'national' social work and International Social Work. Having a part that is not under the sovereignty of nation states in itself, social work has developed an existence beyond nation states not only physically but also conceptually and ideally. It has liberated itself from nation states at least partially. Such terminology as International Social Work of Country A, International Social Work of Country B…is self-contradictory. This form of social work seems to be a newly emerged one but also to be a kind of reversion if one traces back to the origin of social work. The element (being outside of the nation state) seems to have been rooted in social work as if it were its DNA. 'Social work' was born in indigenous[81] localities—although such a term was not used at this time when nations and national borders did not exist or were not in peoples' consciousnesses. Social work emerged under such conditions. Nations were born and national borders were drawn, and eventually embraced social work. (See 2.7 (2) and Figure 3-9, pp.129-131).

International Social Work brings with it its ideas, thoughts, and practices under it in 'national' social work. 'National' social work would become enriched, from the International Social Work point of view, and further social

---

81   See footnote 49 (p.97).

work itself would and will develop onto the next stage,[82] the stage 'of all people' throughout the world.

This new construction is not Chapter 2's 'A Theory of the State' Model (Ch.3 1.1 (2) pp. 94-96) itself but was constructed based on the Mainstream Model in Chapter 2(Ch.3 1.1(1) pp. 92-94), which was mostly based on the understanding and achievements of the international social work of Western-rooted social work, and Chapter 2's State Theory Model which was based on the Mainstream Model and the understanding and achievements of Western-rooted state theories. In this sense, this new structure is also a Western-rooted product and not something that exceeds the understanding and achievements of the Western world, except that the author is from a non-Western, non-English-speaking world, and has a slightly greater respect for the non-Western world.

---

82   The third stage follows the first stage (the birth in Europe) and the second stage (the mutu-ality in North America) as far as Western-rooted professional social work is concerned.

References

Ahmadi, N. (2003). "Globalization and consciousness and new challenges for international social work." *International Journal of Social Welfare*. 12(1). p.14-23.

Akimoto, T. (1992) "Kokusaika to rōdō sōsharu wāku—Genjitsu no kokusaika, shiten no kokusaika, gainen no kokusaika " [Internationalization and labor social work—Internationalization of realities, Internationalization of 'the way of viewing matters,' and Internationalization of the Concept]]. In S. Sato, (Ed.), "Kokusaika Jidai no Fukushi Kadai to Tenbō" [Welfare Issues and Perspectives in Days of Internationalization. Tokyo: Ichiryū sha . 233-249.

Akimoto, T. (1995). "Towards the establishment of an international social work/welfare concept." Unpublished paper. Japan Women's University, Kanagawa, Japan.

Akimoto, T. (1997). "A voice from Japan: Requestioning international social work/welfare: Where are we now? Welfare world and national interest." *Japanese Journal of Social Services*. No.1. Japanese Society for the Study of Social Welfare, Japan. pp.23-34.

Akimoto, T. (2001). "Kokusai Shakai Fukushi" [International Social Work]. In *Encyclopedia of Social Work, Yūhikaku*. pp.1-4.

Akimoto, T. (2004). "The essence of international social work and nine world maps—How to induct students into the secrets of ISW—." In *Social Welfare* (Journal of Social Welfare Department of Japan Women's University). No.45. pp.1-15.

Akimoto, T. (2007)."The Unipolar World and Inequality in Social Work: A response to James Midgley, 'Global inequality, power and the unipolar world: Implications for social work'," *International Social Work*, No. 5, September 2007. 686-690. [Central Conference, The 33rd World Congress of Schools of Social Work, International Association of Schools of Social

Work (IASSW), August 28-31, 2006, Santiago, Chile.]

Akimoto, T. (2007). "Social justice and social welfare policies beyond national boundaries—What Should We Question?" (Proceedings) presented at The 50th Anniversary Celebration of Establishment of Korean Academy of Social Welfare International Conference, "Human Rights and Social Justice: Rethinking Social Welfare's Mission." Seoul University, Seoul, Korea. April 20, 2007. <Reprint> *Shakai Fukushi* [Social Welfare] No. 48. March 2008. <Partial reprint> "Social justice in an era of globalization: must and can it be the focus of social welfare policies?—Japan as a case study." Reich, M. (Ed.). (2016). *Routledge International Handbook of Social Justice*. Routledge.

Akimoto, T. (2017). "Seiyō senmonshoku sōsharu wāku no gurōbarizeshon to bukkyō sōsharu waku no tankyū" [The globalization of Western-rooted professional social work and the exploration of Buddhist social work] In Gohori, J. et al. (Eds.). *Seiyō-umare Senmonshoku Sōsharu Wāku kara Bukkyō Sōsharu Wāku e* [From Western-rooted Professional Social Work to Buddhist Social Work]. ARIISW- Gakubunsha. pp.1-44 (Japanese version: pp.1-53).

Akimoto, T., Fujimori, Y., Gohori, J., Matsuo, K. (2020). "To make social work something truly of the world: Indigenization is not the answer." In Gohori, J. (Ed.) *The Journey of Buddhist Social Work—Exploring the Potential of Buddhism in Asian Social Work*. ARIISW-Shukutoku University. 62-69.

Cox, D. & Pawar, M. (2006) (2013). *International Social Work: Issues, Strategies, and Programs*. Sage Publications, Inc.

Friedlander, W.A. (1975). *International Social Welfare*. Prentice-Hall.

Gohori, J. (Ed.) (2020 and 2021). *The Journey of Buddhist Social Work— Exploring the Potential of Buddhism in Asian Social Work;* and *Social Work Academics Resisting the globalization of Western-rooted Social Work— Decolonization, Indigenization, Spirituality, and Buddhist Social Work*. ARIISW-Shukutoku University.

Healy, L. (1990). [International content in social work education programs worldwide]. Unpublished raw data.

Healy, L. M. (2001). *International Social Work*. Oxford University Press.

Healey, L. & Link, R.J. (Eds.) (2012). *Handbook of International Social Work: Human Rights, Development and the Global Profession*. Oxford University Press.

Hokenstad, T. et al., (1992). *Profiles in International social Work*. NASW Press.

Huegler, N., Lyons, K. & Pawar, M., "1 Setting the Scene." In Lyons, K. et al. (2012).

Hugman, R. (2010). Understanding International Social Work: A Critical Analysis. Basingstoke, Palgrave-Macmillan.

Jebb, E. (1929). "International social service," International Conference of Social Work [Proceedings] (Vo. I, pp.637-655) First Conference, Paris, July 8-13, 1928.

Johnson, H. W. (1996). "International activity in undergraduate social work education in the United States." *International Social Work*. 39(2). pp.189-199.

Kojima, Y. (1992). "Kokusai Shakaifukushi no Kiban" [Foundation of International Social Welfare]. (In Sato, S. (Ed.) *Kokusaika-jidai no Fukushi Kadai to Tenbō* [Welfare Issues and Future in Days of Internationalization. Ichiryūsha. pp.278-303.

Lyons, K. (1999). *International Social Work: Themes and Perspectives*. Ashgate Publishing Limited.

Lyons, K. et al. (2006). "Globalization and social work: International and local implications." *British Journal of Social Work*. 36(3). pp.365-80.

Lyons, K. et al. (2012). *The SAGE Handbook of International Social Work*. Sage Publications.

Nakamura, Y. (1986). "Zadankai: Mokuzen ni Sematta Kokusai Shakaifukushi Kaigi" [A Round-table Talk: Soon Coming International Social Work Conference]. *Gekkan Fukushi* [Monthly Welfare] (1986.4.28).

pp.12-38.

Matsuo, K. (Ed.) (2014). *Internationalization and Indigenization*. ACWelS (Asian Center for Welfare in Societies-Japan College of Social Work).

Matsuo, K., Akimoto, T. and Hattori, M. (Ed.) (2019). "Kokusai Sōsharu-wāku Kyōiku no Karikyuramu wa Ikani Arubeki-ka?" [What Should Curricula for International Social Work Education Be?] (The Third Shukutoku University International Academic Forum, Jan. 20, 2018). Asian Research Institute for International Social Work (ARIISW), Shukutoku University.

Ohno, K. (2000). "Tojōkoku no Gurōbarizeishon—Jiritsu-teki Hatten wa Kanō ka?" [Globalization of Developing Countries—Is Self-sustained Development Possible?]. Tōyō Keizai Shinpōsha.

Payne, M. & Askeland, G. A. (2008). Globalization and International Social Work: Post Modern Change and Challenge. Ashgate Publishing.

Stein, H. (1957, January). "An international perspective in the social work curriculum." paper presented at annual meeting of CSWE, Los Angeles, CA.

Warren, G. (1937). "International social work." In Russell H. Kurtz. (Ed.) *Social Work Year Book*. 4th Issue. New York: Russell Sage Foundation.

Xu, Q. (2006). "Defining international social work: a social service agency perspective". *International Social Work*. 49(6). pp.679-92. 7.

Chapter Four

The Essence of International Social Work and Nine World Maps [83*] —How to Induct Students Into the Secrets of International Social Work—

What is the essence of International Social Work? How can we pass on this essential knowledge to students? This chapter [84*] is a tentative summation of the author's ten-year teaching experience [85*] at Japanese schools of social work.

1. What Is International Social Work?

(1) What International Social Work is not

To practice or conduct research on or in other countries is not equal to international social work. This would be the same if you did this jointly with social work practitioners or professors from other countries. To make an international comparison is not international social work, regardless of drawing lessons for your own country. Comparative analysis is just one of the most basic research methods. To be engaged in practice or research on assistance to the Two-Thirds World is not international social work. This would not change if you refer to "North-South relations."

---

*   marks next to footnote numbers indicate the new insertion on the publication of this book.

83*   This chapter is a reprint of the article (2005) published in Social Welfare (Journal of Social Welfare Department of Japan Women's University) No.45, 2004, with minor corrections and changes. It was originally orally presented at the IASSW (International Association of Schools of Social Work) Board Seminar at Addis Ababa University, Ethiopia, on 20 January 2005.

84*   [In the original] "paper."

85*   Mostly the 1990s.

"Cross-Cultural Social Work" is, of course, not international social work. To devote your energy and talents to international social work organizations such as the IASSW (International Association of Schools of Social Work), the IFSW (International Federation of Social Workers), and the ICSW (International Council on Social Welfare) is not international social work, either. Working with other organizations outside of one's own country is "foreign affairs" activities, which are requisite to almost all kinds of organizations at present. These are all valuable and important but not necessarily international social work (Akimoto, 1997: 26-27) (Ch.2 1 & 2, pp.61-71).

(2) What International Social Work is

What is International Social Work? (a)International Social Work is social work that is concerned with national boundaries.[86*] It is "international" social work. It deals with problems related to or across national boundaries or efforts beyond national boundaries, to solve those problems. (b)International Social Work thinks of and acts for the well-being of all people on this Earth—around eight billion people[87*] in 200 countries and regions—not the well-being of one country or one people. International Social Work is not "national" social work. It is social work beyond the welfare state. (c) International Social Work does not attach any special meaning or importance in value to any specific country or people. It requires not egocentrism and ethnocentrism but "compound eyes". (d)Ignorance and innocence, including those of history, will jeopardize International Social Work both in its practice and research. (Ch.3 2.3 pp.111-116)

The definition or the understanding of international social work has of

---

86*   In Chapter 3, the term "national borders" was mainly used. "National borders" and "national boundaries" have been used interchangeably in this book.

87*   As of 2022. [In the original] "6 billion 4 hundred thousand people.

course changed over time. Period[88*] I occurred around the 1930s, before World War II. There were four ways of breaking national boundaries: serving international social case work (e.g., regarding immigrant and international adoption); internationally assisting disaster and war sufferers and distressed minority groups; holding and attending international conferences; and working for international cooperation in transnational organizations (e.g., the League of Nations, ILO (International Labour Organization) and the International Committee of the Red Cross). They were termed international social work (cf. Warren, 1937: 224 and 1939: 192; Ch.1 1.1, pp.18-22).[89*]

After World War II, aid and assistance to the South by the North became a major form of international social work. This Period II lasted until the 1970s to 80s. The practice and the research on and in other countries or with people of other countries were also considered as international social work. These were other ways to transcend national boundaries. Being engaged in the promotion of international exchange and "foreign affairs" was also termed international social work by some people (Ch.2 1, pp.64-65). We are now in Period III, the next state (Akimoto, 1997:33).

88* [In the original] "Phase". It has been changed to "Period" to conform with the message in Chapter 1. Hereinafter same.

89* Some insertions and changes.

2. How to Convey the Essence of International Social Work

How can we convey the essence of today's international social work mentioned in the two paragraphs above to students in a session or two? [Data on which this section is based are all from classes in Japanese universities. All readers are expected to read the following sections replacing words "Japan" and "Japanese" and Japan-related examples and explanatory descriptions with those of your country, people, and equivalent examples and explanatory descriptions. In Subsection (0) below, Pacific-centred [MAP a] and [MAP b] should be replaced with world maps which are the most commonly used ones in each reader's country. In Subsections (1) to (3), students' perceptions and responses would vary depending on the country or region and/or students' backgrounds. Try the same experimental tests with your students and rewrite paragraphs. The comparative study would be interesting and fruitful.][90*]

(0) Two blank world maps

The first lecture on International Social Work starts with a blank world map [MAP a]. The map is handed to students and instruction is given. "Look at the attached map and write down your feelings and thoughts (20 minutes)."

90*　[　]: New insertion.

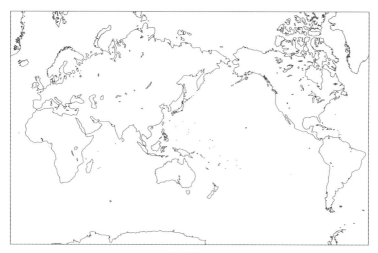

MAP a

Source: https://www.freemap.jp/itemDownload/world/world1/1.png (retrieved 8 Nov. 2022) (replaced the map originally used in classes).

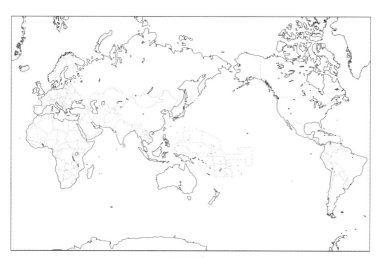

MAP b

Source: https://www.freemap.jp/itemDownload/world/world1/3.png (retrieved 8 Nov. 2022) (replaced the map originally used in classes).

*The dotted lines may not necessarily reflect the actual national border lines. (See 2 (1) below, p.153.) Some countries may not be appropriately represented.

*The height and width ratio of the original maps have been changed by the current author for the page design. (Hereinafter the same, for all following maps.)

Immediately after they are turned in, another blank world map [MAP b] is handed to the students and the same instruction, "Look at the attached map and write down your feelings and thoughts (20 minutes)" is given. The map is the same as the previous map [MAP a] except for the dotted lines drawn on it. From these two maps and their comparison, almost all ingredients, or the essence, of International Social Work can be extracted.

There are four points:

(1) The keyword: National boundaries

The key word, or the core concept, of International Social Work, is a "national boundary." The sole difference between the two maps is the dotted lines. Because of these lines, various problems happen. International Social Work deals with problems caused between and across, and efforts beyond national boundaries to solve those problems.

Generally, for the first map, bright and positive comments tend to be made, as far as Japanese undergraduate students are concerned. For example, "Roomy," "Peaceful," "Unity," "Wholeness," "Conflicts and wars between countries seem to be absurd," "My worries seem to be trivial," and "This Earth is not only for human beings but for all animals and plants." Many refer to seas and continents—their portions, shapes, and historical shifts. For the second map, dark and negative comments tend to be made. For example, "Jumble," "Conflicts and wars," "Strife and feuds," and "Competition and hatred." There are of course some opposite ideas and comments. Attached at the end of the chapter is the list of words, phrases, and sentences given by students. [Appendix, pp.163-173.]

International Social Work is, however, not the social work of the first map. Many practitioners and scholars seem to define international social work as such. They praise words, concepts, and expressions such as an Earthian, a citizen[91] of the world, and a crew member of the spaceship *Planet Earth*. Such understanding, however, encounters criticism as being "superhistorical," unscientific, and irresponsible; ignoring and erasing national boundaries when seeing, thinking, and acting.

We are still in the midst of nation states today, although national boundaries have certainly been broken down in various ways—by goods and services, capital (or multinational corporations), people, information, etc. See the first page of your passport. Japanese passport, for example, reads:

> The Minister for Foreign Affairs of Japan requests all those whom it may concern to allow the bearer, a Japanese national, to pass freely and without hindrance and, in case of need, to afford him or her every possible aid and protection.

The state acts as if it were your "guarantor" or "patron" while you have not asked it to do so. We cannot go anywhere outside our country without a passport.[92*]

Although it may be appropriate to have the concept of a world "citizen" as a long-term goal to which we are directed, we are only somewhere on the way toward this. Seeing the past and the future, we have to know where we are now and think of what we should do. We must always carry the two maps in our pockets, in our minds, in International Social Work. "This is the time when being a good (national) citizen, a good international man/woman, and a good world 'citizen' is called for all simultaneously."

What are national boundaries? When and how were they born? They were man-made and relatively recent in the history of human beings. They are a

---

91 The present concept of "citizens" was constructed in relation to a state in modern Western theories. Citizens have rights to be free from, to demand, and to be entitled to receive services from a state. From whom and to whom are those rights of "citizens of the world"?

92* Except for "within countries under the Schengen Convention," etc.

product of modern nation states. Even today some boundaries have been newly drawn and re-drawn.[93] Some boundaries may be possibly erased or eliminated tomorrow or someday in the future.

(2) The subject: All people on the Earth

International Social Work cares for the wellbeing of all people in this world— eight billion[94*] people in 200 countries and regions—not the well-being of one country or one people. It sees both the Two-Thirds World and One-Third World and their relations. International Social Work is in that sense social work beyond the welfare state, for the welfare state is not only a container of social welfare but also a wall of social welfare. (R. Pinker, 1979) International Social Work can be constructed only on the limitation of the nation-state.

The second map visualizes people's lives in concrete terms. Within the space surrounded by the dotted lines, various people live their lives with and under various political, economic, social, cultural institutions and situations, as well as various natural conditions.

The second map tends to emphasize these variations and differences. International Social Work begins its journey seeking differences. The first map makes us feel the similarities and the commonalities that are not partitioned as in the second map. International Social Work begins a journey seeking commonalities. International Social Work begins journeys in two opposite directions.

More interestingly, viewing the first map again after seeing the second map hints, suggests, and gives the possibility of seeing things not by a

---

93   MAP b, which was a map made in the early days of the 2020s, may not reflect the newest national borders when readers read this book. Some border lines may be new and some others may vanish, which may serve as a good lesson for the understanding of the features and meanings of national borders (rewritten in this publication).

94*   See footnote 106*.

national boundary but by other criteria—such as class, social strata, gender, religion, tribes, and indigenous people/invaders—for analysis and practice, freeing us from the constraints of national boundaries. Not to see the world by country does not mean to see things flatly. To go beyond national boundaries does not mean to make a comparison between and among countries but rather to acquire a way of viewing matters that is not influenced by national boundaries.

(3) 'The way of viewing matters': Not egocentric and ethnocentric but with "compound eyes"—from outside nation states

International Social Work does not give any special position, meaning, or importance in value to any specific country or a specific people. It requires "compound eyes." All International Social Work practitioners and researchers are expected to view things not only with the eyes of their own country but also with the eyes of other countries and the eyes of the whole—not only from the inside but also from the outside.

Almost all students used the word "Japan" or "Japanese" at least once in their answer sheets. They think only from the stance of their own country. A personal sense of belonging is natural and healthy up to a certain level. Few comments were however given from the angle of other countries or peoples.

One assignment I gave in a class in May 2004 was the following: "Three Japanese nationals [a freelance photographer, a freelance writer, and a volunteer child welfare activist who were critical of the Japanese government's dispatch of the Self-Defense Forces of Japan to support the United States Iraq war and were in Iraq for humanitarian assistance, ignoring the Japanese government's 'advisory recommending evacuation',[95*]] have been kidnapped [by an Iraqi armed group]. Map the feelings, the understanding,

---

95*   A new insertion.

the thoughts, and responses of the various players or stakeholders." The three hostages, their families, their friends, the organizations they belonged to, the Japanese government, the United States government, the Iraqi government and various other governments, NGOs, the general public in various countries, their sub-populations, various segments of Iraqi people, and many others...The question itself had a fundamental flaw. Why wasn't it phrased as "We kidnapped three Japanese," or in the active voice?

On the other hand, many students pointed out that the two maps were Japanese world maps because Japan was located in the centre. There are typically three kinds of world maps today—the "East Asian countries/the Pacific Ocean-centred world map [MAP c]," the authentic "European world map [MAP d]," and the "American world map [MAP e]." How "arrogant" they are! (Not only that of Eastern Asian countries but also of the other countries.) They put their own countries in the middle. Particularly, the "American world map" bravely cuts the Eurasian Continent in half, putting

MAP c
Source: Waido Sekai Zenzu [Wide World Map]. To–bunsha, Tokyo.

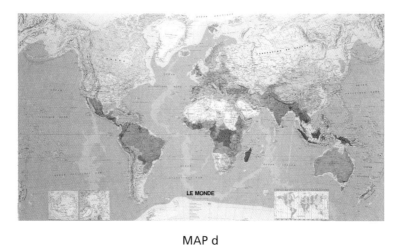

MAP d

Source: LE MONDE. Projection Van der Grinten mondifiée MICHELEN.

* The original map had national flags around it but they were trimmed away by the author.

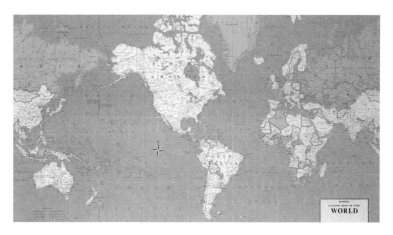

MAP e

Source: Classic Map of the World (HAMMOND Incorporated. Mamplewood. NJ).

*The height and width ratio of the original maps (MAPs c, d, and e) have been changed by the current author for the page design.

its eastern half on the west side and its western half on the east side.

In addition to egocentrism, the emphasis on the theory of the elite and the superiority of one's own, e.g., Sino centrism, Zionism, the elite and the superiority of the Germanic people, the Japanese, and the Anglo-Saxons,[96] seems to be a common character of all countries. These are on pole opposite to International Social Work.

A map is a dangerous thing. It can control your way of thinking about and seeing the world. Not only among countries but also in North-South relations, a severe bias has been infused. The equator was not located at the centre of the three maps above. The North has been unproportionally magnified. Peters' Projection [MAP f] is a challenge to this bias although the part at the very top is still drawn disproportionately wide.[97] Both at the national level and also at the individual level, discriminatory, superior, or disdainful views are baneful.

---

96   People may define each of these terms or concepts differently, sometimes positively and
     sometimes negatively.
97   This is unavoidable when we use a plane to represent the surface of a sphere.

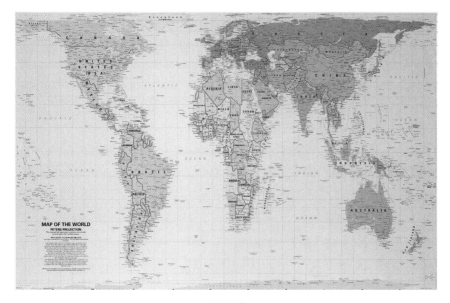

MAP f
Source: World View, Peters Projection Map (WorldView Publications: Oxford, UK).
*The height and width ratio of the original map have been changed by the current author for the page design.

(4) The preparation: Overcoming ignorance and innocence

Ignorance and innocence as well as popular beliefs are fatally detrimental to International Social Work in its practice and research. Some examples:

(a) Looking at the two blank world maps, many Japanese students start their comments with "Japan is a small island country" in their answer sheets. The notion has been a persistently prevailing common knowledge in Japan. Is Japan small? Yes, but how small is it among all countries in the world? Japan is the 60th biggest among some 194 countries and regions, according to a data book (Ninomiya Shoten, 2001: 18-24)—a third from the top. There are only three countries in Europe that are bigger than Japan: France, Spain, and

157

Sweden. Japan is the 11th[98*] largest in population, and 6th or 8th biggest, depending on the source, in terms of area (with its Exclusive Economic Zone considered). Can we discuss International Social Work with this misperception? Japan is an island country. Yes, but so what? So it has an island country mentality, that is, an insular spirit. It is narrow-minded. There are many island countries in the world—Iceland, the United Kingdom, Cyprus, Madagascar, Qatar, Cuba, Jamaica, New Zealand, Papua New Guinea, Sri Lanka, Tuvalu, Philippines, Indonesia…Do they share the same insularity?

(b) [MAP g] is a 1507 map obtained at the Vatican. Where can we find Japan? "Nowhere," responded a sales staff member wearing a robe, who was

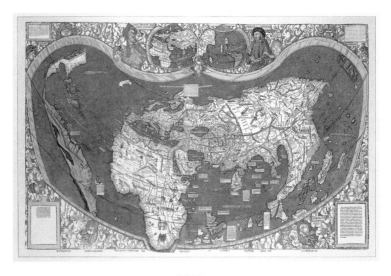

MAP g
Source: Waldseemiiller's World Map, 1507 (Wychwood Editions).
*The height and width ratio of the original map have been changed by the current author for the page design.

98*　UNFPA State of World Population 2022 [In the original text, Japan was 9th] .

attending the display desk.[99]* What does this mean? There are two serious implications. One, in the brains and minds of the people who made and used this map, Japan—where millions of human beings were living—did not exist. Their world was different from the reality. Two, how do people feel about being ignored? Maybe not comfortable. To put it bluntly, it is a form of conceptual genocide. How terrible this is! Users as well as cartographers crossed out millions of people's existence.

The next assignment to students was "Simply write as many country names as possible (15 minutes)." To be shameful, the Japanese college students in my classes were able to write only around 60 country names on average (the maximum was 137), a third of all existing countries. What does this mean? Can you practice and study International Social Work with so little knowledge?

(c) [MAP h] is hard for the author to display in front of people, especially Asian colleagues. Taiwan, the Korean Peninsula, and some Pacific islands are painted red as in Japan, and the northeastern part of China is orange. This is a map taken from an atlas published in 1939 and is proof of Japanese imperialism, colonialism, and aggression. Few students had seen this map. Although many said they knew the historical facts, they could not imagine what had really happened because it was all in the distant past, from their perspective. To these young people, it didn't personally involve them and wasn't a part of their life.

---

99   I am not sure if the answer was correct or not. A small island at the east end may be intended to be Japan without identification.

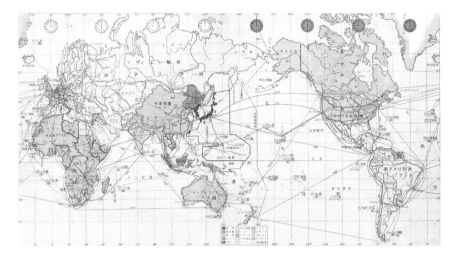

MAP h

Source: *Shinsen Dai-chizu,Nippon-hen* [New Atlas: Japan] Michio Moriya,
(Teikoku Shoin. Tokyo, 1939) pp. 2-3.

*The original map had colours and weather signal flags around it but they were trimmed away by the author.

*The height and width ratio of the original map have been changed by the current author for the page design.

On the other hand, many students do seem to have innocently no discriminatory feelings against the people of those countries that Japan once invaded, at least at the conscious level. They become friends with young people[100*] of those countries without hesitation while older generations[101*] have some conflicting feelings regardless of their political or ideological position— reactionaries, conservatives, liberalists, or radicals. "We had not even been born during that period of aggression," say young students, implying that they are not responsible for history. Is this excuse acceptable for those whose countries were once invaded?[102] Can you practice or research International

---

100* Remember that the original article of this chapter was written at the beginning of the 2000s.

101* Remember that the original article of this chapter was written at the beginning of the 2000s.

102 "You are enjoying an affluent life as a historical inheritance. We must inherit our history as a whole."

Social Work with this innocence? "It is not only Japan that invaded, killed, and exploited" other countries, say some people. But it is a fact Japan did. It is not easy for a Japanese to work in Asia.[103*]

(d) Asian countries are our neighbours. Is this commonly accepted view correct? There is a field named Telegeography. At one time, a map drawn by the volume of telephone and facsimile[104*] communication (1990-91) was presented in an article in a journal. (Staple, 1994: 29)[105*] ["MAP i Japan Communication Continent" (omitted)]. The proportion of the space of Japan covered by Country A (e.g. 23% in the case of the US) shows the volume of the information sent to the country among all the information sent out to all countries from Japan, and the proportion of Japan in the space of Country A (e.g. 4% in case of the US) shows the volume of the information sent to Japan among all the information Country A sent out to all countries. Neighbouring countries for Japan seem to be North American countries and European Community countries, but not Asian countries.[106*] Most Asian countries are distantly located. Are we ready for International Social Work?

Chapter Four

There is no need to summarize this short story to this point. Please make an equivalent story, replacing "Japan" and "Japanese" with your own country and your own people, and think and practice.

103* Akimoto, T. (2003). One-page policy statement was distributed when the current author ran for Board Member-at-large in the 2003 IASSW election.
104* Today Internet communication, which was not so common at the beginning of the 90s, would be even more important and the map might be significantly different.
105* The proceeding two sentences have been slightly changed.
106* The proportion has significantly changed in these few decades.

References

Akimoto, T. (1995). "A Voice from Japan: Requestioning International Social Work/Welfare: Where Are We Now?" *Japanese Journal of Social Services*, No. 1. October, pp.23- 34.

Ninomiya Shoten (2001). *Data Book of the World*, Vol.13.

*Pinker, R. (1979). *The Idea of Welfare*. London: Heinemann.

*Staple. C.G. (1994). "Terejiogurafi kara mita sekai" [The world seen from Telegiography]. *The TeleGiograpy*. 25-32. Cf. *TeleGiograpy*, (yearbook). International Institute of Communications and TeleGeography, Inc.

*Warren, G. (1937 and 1939). "International social work." In R. Kurtz, (Ed.), *Social Work Yearbook*. Vol. 4 and 5. New York: Russell Sage Foundation. 224-227 and 192-196 respectively.

* New insertions for this chapter. They were not included in the original article reprinted for this chapter.

[Appendix] Two blank world maps

The following comments, grouped by topic (e.g., "A small island country"), were given by 38 undergraduate students, mainly sophomores and juniors, in the first session of the 2004 International Social Work class of Japan Women's University, Tokyo, Japan.

Two blank maps were handed to students and the following instructions were given. "Look at the attached maps and write down your feelings and thoughts about them within 20 minutes." (See pp.148 and 150).

Students have not learned about international social work yet. These comments are similar to those given by students in other classes at Japan Women's University and other universities in the Tokyo area in the past ten years. See Section 2. (0) and (1) (particularly, its first and second paragraphs, pp.150-151) of Chapter 4. Also see the first paragraph of Section 2, Chapter 4, p.148.

Comments about both maps [MAP a & MAP b]

"A small island country"

1. Japan is a small island country.

   Japan is really small.

   How small Japan is!

2. Island countries are few.

   I feel insecure about the lack of links with other countries.

3. It's a great matter that Japan is a world economic power while it is really small.

"Japanese world map"

4. This is a Japan-centered world map.

   Probably Japanese made it.

   It's natural to put your own country in the middle, but I sense some egocentrism—Japanese supremacy.

What do world maps in other countries look like?

5. It's rather unnatural to put France or the United States in the middle while we are Japanese. It's important to love your own country.

Comments about the first map [MAP a]

"Broad and spacious and peaceful"

1. Broad, spacious, open.

   I feel refreshed.

2. Peaceful.

   What trivial matters we fight over!

   Wars and strife between states seem absurd.

"Unity and a whole"

3. The world looks to be one.

   I feel intimacy with all of it.

   I feel I could go anywhere just now.

   I don't feel the distance between countries.

   All countries look alike although they have been partitioned and have their own cultures and policies.

   Some places are now at war and others at peace and some places are poor and others are wealthy, aren't they?

4. Without national boundaries, not an end but continuity is seen between Europe and the Middle East.

"Continents"

5. Not countries but continents come to our eyes.

6. The shapes of the continents are interesting.

   All continents fit each other to make a big continent.

   Once upon a time, all continents were connected, people say.

   The phrase:

"All people are brothers and sisters" comes to mind.

7. The Earth is made of land and sea.

   The oceans look much bigger than the land. .

   The Pacific Ocean is huge.

   Is this how the Arabian Peninsula and the Mediterranean Sea were always shaped?

8. Some parts of today's land may disappear in the future due to global warming, and the area of seas and oceans may become larger.

   Environmental problems should be discussed more as the world is connected into one.

"Six billion [sic][107*] people and not for human beings alone"

9. Are people living on small islands in an ocean? If yes, how are they living? In each place, many kinds of people are living different lives. How wonderful it is for those people to live at the same time on the same Earth with their respective norms and standards.

10. The world population has exceeded six billion.[108*]

11. This Earth belongs not only to human beings but also to animals and other life.

12. The world is certainly big, but the universe is much bigger.

"My existence and my worry"

13. Here I am living in this universe, just like one little speck of dust, worrying and struggling. The whole idea seems comical in a way.

    "I" could be dotted on this map only with a precision instrument. It's pitiably cute for a human being to strive over such a tiny life. My worry seems to be a very small matter.

"Part of a whole"

14. All countries are on this one planet and connected by land and sea.

107* As of the beginning of the 2000s when the original article was written. Now (2023), it should be replaced with "eight billion."

108* Ditto.

The world is linked together.

15. Japan is small and part of the large world.

16. This map presents only the essential framework of the world before us.

Why has what used to be one come apart?

"Poverty"

17. How many people are living happy lives with sufficient living standards now?

The gap between the rich and the poor is huge even though we are on the same Earth: Why?

18. Japan is full of goods but there are also poor countries in the same Asia.

Every day, thousands of thousands starve to death.

19. Somewhere far from or very near to us, many people on this map have no security, not even the assurance of a daily meal.

In Japan, too, some people are homeless and don't know where their next meal is coming from.

"Wars & conflicts"

20. We have wars and troubles right now somewhere.

Iraq is at war[109*] and many other places I don't know have poor security.

Many people have become victims.

"National boundaries & states"

21. There might be no wars without national boundaries.

Nationality changes and laws and institutions all become different once you cross a national border even by one centimetre.

22. There may be no need for us to have the unit of a "state." Because of a "state," nationalism sprouts, and the distance between "our" country and "their" countries is born while all states are on the same continents of the Earth. This has produced wars, discrimination, poverty, etc. In terms of social welfare, we think of that of our own country even though society is

---

109* The original article of this chapter was written in early years of the 2000s.

composed of all continents on this Earth.

23. We call people from other countries *"Gaijin"* (Foreigners. strangers, aliens, or outsiders). This is a discriminatory term or a carryover from 400 years of national seclusion. It sounds as if we were rejecting them.

24. It is necessary to know about Japan if we want to bring up true "international men and women."

25. The world is one. The Japanese, the Americans, and the people of Africa are really all one race: the human race…race is not important. I would like to say so. But it would be whitewashing. The culture and religion of each district and country, which have been built up through history, have become sources of trouble, produced many victims, making mutual understanding among people difficult. Seeing and hearing recent Iraqi related incidents and news. I have been convinced that I, a pacifist, and those who want to "solve" the problem with war and force have no common words and could never reach a mutual understanding. The only commonality among us is the simple fact that we are all human beings who are living on this map. There is nothing else to share. Everything else is quite different

"Perception"

26. The Japanese do not seem to be proud of being part of Asia although we are part of Asia. They yearn for the character of Europe of which they have nothing in common (not hair colour, skin colour or temperament). Japanese are attracted even by the sound of the word, "Europe" itself. How about other Asian people? Do they also revere Europe? How do the Europeans perceive Asians? What does Japan, a small country, look like in their eyes?

"Modesty"

27. The world I know is just part of the whole.

I only know something about tiny Japan.

There are many places and countries that I don't know.

With this poor knowledge can I study International Social Work?

28. There are people live in totally different environments and have different customs. It's important to know of them.

29. The world is big and each country has various problems which I really know nothing about. I wish I had taken an interest in them.

It's necessary to see various countries and places.

30. Watching the news about Iraqi problems, I am little concerned with them, while they have happened within a distance of only ten centimetres on this small scale of a map.

What percentage of people in this world lack basic necessities--clothes, food, and houses?

Even now many people are involved in wars and violent incidents somewhere. But I don't know nor do try to know even where. I am only concerned with something around myself. I feel I am very a small person.

"Aspiration"

31. I live in a small city in the small country of Japan and there's a lot that I haven't seen, yet I would like to see and know more.

I want to see as many people as possible.

32. I want to get out of this small Japan into the big world to have various experiences.

Other comments

33. Europe seems smaller than I thought. It is unbelievable for me that countries in such a small Europe had the power to divide the world.

34. The closeness between countries does not depend on the distance.

35. All the talk about globalization seems trivial when we look at tiny maps like these.

36. Until when will Japan be ruled and controlled by the United States even while we are located far from each other? I feel uneasy.

37. I wonder if the world will rain ruin on itself someday.

Comments about the second map [MAP b]

"Narrow, cramped and closed"

1. Jumbled.

   How narrow the world is!

   Only with national boundaries added, the world looks smaller. I am choked with being cramped.

   Crowded.

   Closed.

2. The feeling of liberation in the first map has gone somewhere.

3. The map with national boundaries seems unnatural. The map without them seemed better.

4. I am somehow sad with this map, particularly after looking at the first map.

5. Dotted lines are unpleasant.

   They look like a patchwork of dinosaur skeletons.

"Piecemeal"

6. The world has been divided into small bits and each of them has been fenced. Seas are also divided into territorial waters. The world is more fragmented.

7. If people live in a smaller divided space, the world they think of also becomes smaller.

8. The world looked to be one in the first map but it's now firmly divided.

   The world looks like not one but an aggregate of various countries.

"National boundaries"

9. In this map, there are national boundaries.

   We are accustomed to this map with national boundaries that were artificially drawn.

   Everything would differ if we went a step beyond a national boundary.

   You would feel foreign unreasonably.

10. I feel the distance between countries.

11. What is a national boundary? How was it decided? What was used as a basis for the decision?

    What meaning was there in drawing the line?

    Shapes of countries have been drawn by the hands of men/women, except for island countries like Japan.

12. Why did shapes become so complicated as these?

    Why aren't the lines straight? It would be easier to handle this with straight lines.

13. It is apparent that the straight border lines were drawn artificially by people.

14. The national boundary lines in Africa are frightening, and tell the history of competing European countries' invasions.

    I feel very sad. Borderlines in Africa make me disconsolate.

    I learned in schools that many of the national boundaries in Africa were decided by European and American countries without consideration for tribal or religious relations.

    Thinking about whose colony each country was, I feel the cruelty afresh One nation should never rule another.

15. How different are the people on both sides near a border?

16. On one hand, there are many people who aren't convinced by the present map lines, and on the other hand, there are many people who don't care about them.

17. The meaning of national boundaries would be different in Japan, an island country, and in Europe and America where many countries are closely located.

    How do people feel in a country immediately neighbouring other countries?

    How do people feel with people on the other side of the borderline whose language, food, and buildings are different?

"A state"

18. National boundaries expel the view of continents.

   The world grasped by a state is presented rather than the world by a continent.

   The relationship between states, being good or bad, comes to the fore.

19. With national boundaries, human beings made distances between themselves by themselves.

   People became unable to come and go freely anymore. Always distinguishing you from others and putting them far from you, people won't walk toward each other.

   The strong insistence of a state drives people not to cross dotted lines and to accept what exists only within the border to reject all others from horror.

20. Without national boundaries, we think of "people living in the same world." With national boundaries, we distinguish people of our country and people of other countries, e.g., Japanese and foreigners.

"Wars, conflicts, struggles, competition and hatred"

21. It's strange—being divided by dotted lines, states now start insisting on their rights and territories.

   Many countries competed, hated, and repeatedly fought each other. It's too sad when they are neighbours.

   National boundaries remind me of many wars over land. I heard many tragic stories about national borders.

22. Seeing wars in the past and territory disputes today, human beings seem to be creatures that always want to expand their territories. For me what's important is how more people become happier rather than how more territory is obtained. The size of a country is not the determinant of affluence.

23. Human beings have repeated wars over national boundaries for many centuries. Japan also invaded other countries before and during World

War II to expand its territory, but I cannot help wondering why people stick to their national boundaries. territories and interests. People will probably continue fighting for them forever.

24. People have been afflicted by the national boundaries that they made, haven't they?

Many people have suffered with national boundaries.

25. It does not seem to be important to me which countries are strong and which countries are weak.

The world looks flat: I don't feel the difference between rich and poor on this map.

26. In the name of religion, people killed each other. Is belief in a religion justifiable for killing people?

"The shape and the size of countries"

27. Big countries, small countries, and countries like particles.

A country like a dot or a huge country like Russia is equally a country.

The size of the land does not parallel the affluence of the country.

28. I am tempted to put in colours.

29. There are many countries in Africa.

There are more countries in the Southern Hemisphere.

The Southern Hemisphere contains many "developing countries" in it.

30. Racial discrimination is firmly rooted but countries of Blacks, Whites, and Yellows are roughly the same in number and area. It is unreasonable and unfair to discriminate against each other.

"Visualization"

31. Each country is now spending time at its own pace, ways, and values.

32. The actual lives of people, e.g. special products, folk costumes, and animals, can be visualized.

I can imagine the politics, laws, cultures, religions, and languages in each country.

What do people eat for breakfast in each area surrounded by lines? The difference in characters by region interests me.

33. Since cultures, races, and others differ, the world may be interesting, but in reality, the differences have sadly caused conflicts.

"Aspiration"

34. I have been to some countries but haven't been to many.

   I have started thinking that I want to go this country or that island.

   I would like to travel to many places.

"Erasing national boundaries"

35. Lines of national boundaries are obstacles.

   I think national boundaries are unnecessary. Their value has been disappearing in this time of internationalization, globalization, and the information society.

36. Various new phenomena beyond national boundaries have been occurring, e.g., the destruction of nature.

   National boundaries have reached a limit today. We have to strive for the solution of the problems on a global scale.

37. I wish all these lines would vanish someday from this world.

38. What if there were no national boundaries? I am curious.

   I am fearful. I have a hunch that the worst thing would happen.

39. Dotted lines cannot be erased so easily. They seem to have existed from the old days.

40. The problem for us is how to overcome the concept of a "state."

Other comments

41. Besides national boundaries, many invisible borders have not been shown here in the world. Human beings are creatures that want to create "borders" from ancient times.

42. Many common problems exist within each dotted line such as the gap between the extremely rich and poor and wars and racial conflicts.

43. It is great that English is the common language of the world. But I wonder if it is good or not for all people to be able to speak English.

Postface

The reason for this publication

Discussion held in this book was at the conceptual level. The book was originally compiled and directed towards leading veteran international social work theorists, researchers, educators, and practitioners around the world. This new International Social Work, however, ought not to interest or be accepted among most of them and their followers, who are based on the equation "social work = Western-rooted (professional) social work." That is fine. The author truly respects them and their international social work.

The author's intention in this book is not the redefinition and the reconstruction of their international social work, but the construction of a new international social work. The newly-constructed International Social Work is that of* all eight billion people in the world. It concerns them equally, and their wellbeing, difficulties, and problems in life, i.e., "social work needs" in the words of Western-rooted social work. Western-rooted (professional) social work has served and will be able to serve only part of them, in quality and quantity.

A few clues to understand the new International Social Work

Through test discussions, lectures, and reading in the process of writing, editing, reviewing, and printing, the new International Social Work found newcomers to its field to be interested in it and to easily understand and accept it when the following few clues were given.

1. Its locational relation to Western-rooted professional social work: The new International Social Work is located outside Western-rooted (professional) social work while embracing it as described above (cf. p178). The new International Social Work is not based on the equation that 'social work' is equal to 'Western-rooted social work,' which was assumed to be born through the industrialization, at the end of 19th century, or after "charity."

Otherwise, the overwhelming majority of people would be left outside social work. International Social Work must have affinity with and be coexistent with all kinds of social work, not only Western-rooted (professional) social work. Most of those kinds of social work do not or may not, of course, use the term "social work", particularly in English, for themselves.

2. Its standing position in relation to sovereign nations: It is also located outside sovereign states while always keeping them in mind. Social work had supposedly existed before national borders, in consciousness or in reality, and gradually shifted its functions to states, eventually to be embraced by them. Part of the social work spun off from them as international social work, to become an entity outside their sovereignty while remaining within social work. International social work views matters from and for the whole, not from and for respective national interests. Social work itself resumed the view before national borders with such International Social Work included in it (Chapter 3 2.7 (2) p.129).

3. The explicit distinction between social work and social workers: What the new International Social Work discussed was not on social workers and their activities/functions, but on social work, which was the subject of our research. Also, the distinction has been consciously made between (professional) social workers and those who do social work regardless of whether it is their occupation or not.

In addition, to understand the new International Social Work, the following basic preparative knowledge (primitive theories beyond the social work discipline and simple statistical facts) is necessary: 1. the birth, growth, and change of nation (sovereign) states and national borders; 2. the relation among nationalism, internationalism, and cosmopolitanism; 3. language

---

*   The title of the book has intentionally adopted "of" neither "for" nor "by".

issues and policies; 4. the geographic distribution and the diversity of people; 5. the geographic distribution of (professional) social workers on the Earth; and 6. various other knowledge.

Some dilemmas to be tackled—the expectation to future generations

The discussion of this book has been uncompleted. Some discussion has been expected to the next generations.

1. While International Social Work was defined to free it from bonds to sovereign nations, those who practice it have not been freed from nationalities. How to accommodate this dilemma? To become a no-nationality person for oneself is usually not allowed, nor is it easy.

2. While the orientation to "welfare world" after "welfare state" was proposed, the theoretical development of its idea and/or its alternative ideas in this half a century has not been reviewed nor considered in this book.

3. While the construction of International Social Work of all people on this earth would be possible only being based on all kinds of indigenous (cf. Ch.3 1.1 (2) footnote 49, p.97) social work in the world, those indigenous kinds of social work have not been conscientized, discussed, and constructed as social work yet. The only social work that has been revealed in a systematized tangible form today is Western-rooted (professional) social work.

4. The 'value' (human rights, social justice, democracy, etc.) which the international social work of the Western-rooted (professional) social work takes for granted was replaced with 'the way of viewing matters' in the new International Social Work. This new International Social Work aims to eliminate or minimize the value factor as much as possible for (international) social work to be a scientific discipline and deal with or skirt around both the current dysfunctional United Nations and the conflict-ridden international society. However, if e.g., "the view from the

176

outside (of nation states)" is thrown in to fill the content of 'the way of viewing matters,' it might be still deemed to be a value.

5. This book attempted to construct a new international social work, but the product is far from what the author dreamed of. This book started with the literature review of international social work of Western-rooted professional social work (and only that by English-speaking people), listened to people from the non-Western, non-English world, and made a new proposal applying a kind of 'a theory of the State.' But the 'state theory' was also Western-rooted. In this sense, this new International Social Work is also a Western-rooted product, and not one that exceeds the understandings and achievements of the Western world, except that the author is from a non-Western, non-English-speaking world and that a little heavier respect was given to the non-Western world. No matter how far Sun Wu-K'ung flew, he could not escape from the palm of the Buddha's hand. Someday someone will hopefully construct the real international social work based on and applicable for the whole population, or all societies and countries and regions, on this planet.

At last, the most important inquiry on practice now is how the practices (including policy, etc.) that readers have been currently engaged in under the Western-rooted (professional) social work would alter or not alter if they take this new interpretation of international social work. We expect our future generations to obtain the proof positive and its record. Meanwhile, if we suppose that this International Social Work must spread into the mainstream social work community, one strategically effective route might be how to connect and lead 'international social work (A)' to 'international social work (B)' (Chapter 3 2.2 (1) pp.108 and 110).

Is the concept of international social work—and thus, social work—effective without an understanding of this book, in the current war-ridden world?

Deciphering the new International Social Work

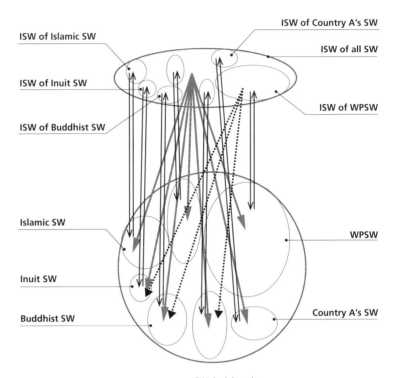

SW: Social work
NSW: 'National' social work
ISW: International Social Work
WPSW: Western-rooted professional social work

1. International social work of Western-rooted professional social work can serve only part of the whole.

2. International social work of the social work which was born and grew in a certain culture and society could work effectively in that culture and society, but couldn't in the different culture and society on which it is not based.

3. The new International Social Work has affinity for all social work and compatibility in all cultures and societies.

Index

compassion 131
"compound eyes" 8, 15, 91, 95, 146, 153
Conference (1928)
    the first international social work
    conference in Paris 18
conflict prevention 31, 32
constituency 8, 91, 113, 132-4, 136
constituents 113
container but also a wall 74
convention 58, 72, 114, 121, 135
Convention on the Rights of the Child 124
Convention on the Rights of Persons with
    Disabilities 124
Cooperative for Assistance and Relief
    Everywhere International (CARE) 65
cosmopolitan 77, 81, 136
cosmopolitanism 19, 58, 175
Council on Social Work Education (CSWE)
    24
country-by-country social work 14
Cox, D. 16, 31-3, 42, 46, 53, 102, 142
crew member of the spaceship Planet Earth
    151
cross-cultural counselling 44, 64
cross-cultural social work 53, 55, 64, 146
cross-cultural understanding 25
cross-national 30, 38, 45, 79, 135
CSWE 24, 53
cultural boundaries 24, 112
cultural imperialism 27
cultural perspective 43, 44
culture 35, 39, 59, 70, 103, 104, 106, 107, 122,
    164, 167, 172

D

democracy 14, 31, 43, 46, 90, 94, 176
development (social; economic) 29, 31, 33,
    39, 40, 43, 46, 57, 58, 60, 62, 75, 144
developmental assistance 66
developmental stage 14, 40, 75, 83
dialectically 31, 32, 36
different cultures 36, 64
difficulties and problems in (people's) live(s)
    112, 113, 174
disappearance of international social work
    49
disaster 21, 40, 93, 147

sufferers 21
dissemination of social work 23
disseminating social work 41
distressed minority groups 21, 40, 147
DNA molecule 130
domestic 8, 13, 27, 29, 36, 68, 72, 80, 93, 117,
    134, 137
    practice and advocacy 29
domestic interference 72, 78, 126
domestic social work (practice) 13, 14, 36,
    46, 67-71, 108
Dominelli, L. 38, 53

E

Earthians 115
East-West relations (relationship) 22, 42, 44,
    45
Ecological perspectives 33
ecology 31, 33, 46
economic expansion 7, 81
egocentrism 146, 156, 164
elite and the superiority of 155
Elliott, D. 53
embrace 96, 107
emergency relief activities 66
Encyclopedia of Social Work 20, 62, 65, 71
end of 19th century 174
English-medium 7, 51
English-speaking 7, 51, 177
environment protection 79
equality 47, 73, 77
erasure of national boundaries/borders 81,
    136
essence of international social work 9, 82,
    141, 145, 148, 150
ethical 107
    guidelines 32
    practice 36
ethics 14, 27, 31, 45
EU (European Union) 78-80
exchange
    of information, knowledge, ideas, skills,
    and model 19, 21, 26, 40, 64, 65, 93
eyes (views) from the outside 91, 95, 113,
    132, 133, 136

R

radical social work 54
Ramanathan, C. S. 36,54
Rebecca, L. T. 17
Red Cross 18, 41, 50, 65, 93, 110, 147
redefinition 174
reformist approach 23
refugee 24, 28, 29, 64, 70, 72, 78
    regional associations 23
religion 77, 115, 153, 167, 172
resolutions and declarations 72
Rinen 12, 116
roles and functions of international social
    work 38, 49, 50, 100
Romanyshyn, J.M. 66, 86
Rousseau, J-J. 14, 95

S

Sakamoto, E. 103
Sasaki, A. 103
Sanders, D. 24, 55, 66, 86, 104, 105, 112
Save the Children 18, 40, 50, 93, 110
self-sufficient, closed system 121
shakai-fukushi, 57
Simpson, G. 54
Sino centrism 156
sister city program 65
small island country 157, 163
social care 131
social development 31, 33, 57, 75
social justice 14, 31, 32, 35, 37, 43, 45, 48, 72,
    90, 93, 94, 98, 112, 114, 142, 176
social problems 23, 34-7, 49
social strata 153
social welfare 7, 25, 29, 48, 57, 60-3, 65-7, 69,
    72, 74, 75, 79, 80, 145, 146, 152, 166
social work and social workers 88, 99, 175
social work as a whole 8, 98, 101, 110, 111,
    116, 133
social work by country 97
social work by government 130
social work's capacity 33
social work colonialism 26, 47
social work imperialism 126
social work internationalism 38

social work needs 35, 174
Social Work Year Book 40, 43, 65, 66, 71, 86,
    87, 144, 162
'social work = professional social work' 102,
    174
social work = Western-rooted (professional)
    social work 8, 99, 138
socialism vs. capitalism 23
socially disadvantaged 71
sovereign countries 8
sovereign nation 8, 9, 95, 104, 106, 108, 112,
    116, 128, 139, 175, 176
sovereignty 9, 91, 96, 105, 106, 116, 118, 122,
    130, 139, 175
spin(-)off 117, 118, 131
Spinoza, B. 14, 95
Spirituality 142
Stage I 102
Stage II 102
Stage III 102
standard(s) 14, 15, 17, 27, 31, 34, 35, 43, 45,
    46, 48, 49, 58, 77, 90, 94, 101, 113, 124, 129,
    133, 134, 165, 166
state social work 13, 14, 108, 130, 131
Stein, H. 25, 55, 144
subject(s) 32, 33, 47, 64, 68, 81, 104, 106, 153
Sun Wu-K'ung 177
supra-national 38

T

(TA) 17, 20, 22, 23, 26, 27, 34, 36
target population 32, 89, 113
Telegeography 161, 162
Ten Christian Commandments 131
tentative definition 58, 75
"theory of the State" 14, 58, 88, 94, 95, 107,
    136, 177
'theory of the state' model 90, 94, 102, 140
Thomas, R. 16, 17, 53
third stage 50, 101, 117, 140
torch 128, 139
transfer and the assistance
    from the North to the South 22
transfer
    of information, knowledge, ideas, skills,
    and model 48
transnational fostering 36

transnational organizations 147
trans- or inter-governmental organizations 134
tribes 153
Two-Thirds World 62, 66, 145, 152

U

UNESCO 133, 134
UNFPA 158
UNICEF 50, 65
unidirectional 26, 43, 44, 46-8
relationship 45
unipolar theory 126, 141
United Nations 8, 22-4, 50, 58, 62, 65, 66, 70, 72, 73, 76, 78, 79, 97, 114, 115, 121, 128, 137, 176
United Nations Children's (Emergency) Fund (UNICEF) 65
United States 20, 22-4, 51, 59, 62, 67, 68, 70, 78, 153, 154, 164, 168
United States Children's Bureau 65
United Kingdom 22, 23, 51, 69, 158

V

value 8, 14, 33, 43, 47, 48, 72, 90, 93, 137, 146, 153, 173, 176, 177
'value' 27, 31-3, 37, 45-8, 88, 89, 95, 98, 126, 176
value-driven action 34
'value' elements 49, 98
value-focused definition 31, 33, 43, 46, 48, 49, 98, 99
value (judgmental) factor 18, 31, 34, 42, 46, 47, 114
'value' = 'human rights and social justice' 37, 176
various (other) types of social work 8, 127, 138
Vasudevan, V. 50, 56
view from the outside 9, 15, 176
voluntary work without expecting returns 131

W

war orphans 64

war sufferers 21, 147
Warren, G. 18, 21, 28, 40, 42, 55, 66, 87, 93, 144, 147, 162
Watts, T. D. 53
way of viewing matters 8, 12, 14, 15, 57, 58, 60, 71, 75-8, 82, 83, 88, 89, 91, 95, 98, 101, 113, 114, 117, 126, 132-4, 153, 176, 177
Webb, S. A. 39, 55
welfare state 14, 58, 73, 74,77, 83, 91, 94-6, 130, 131, 136, 146, 152, 176
welfare world 14, 58, 60, 73-8, 80-3, 91, 94, 136, 141, 176
well-being 57, 110, 113, 114, 132, 146, 152
human 29, 34
social 75
Western Europe 107
Westernization 126, 137
Western or Northern powers 23
WHO 65, 135
working committee, CSWE's 24
World Health Organization (WHO) 65
world state 80, 128
world welfare 80

X

Xu, Q. 16, 18, 55, 144

Y

yardstick 15, 113, 121, 124, 129, 131-4, 136
Yamato race 115

Z

Zionism 156

INTERNATIONAL
SOCIAL WORK
of All People in the Whole World

A New Construction

2024 年 2 月 10 日　初版第 1 刷発行

著者
秋元　樹

デザイン
坂野公一
（welle design）

発行者
淑徳大学アジア国際社会福祉研究所

制作・発売
株式会社 旬報社
〒 162-0041 東京都新宿区早稲田鶴巻町 544
TEL 03-5579-8973　FAX 03-5579-8975
ホームページ https://www.junposha.com/

印刷・製本
中央精版印刷株式会社